OUR WAY HOME

OUR WAY HOME

A Journey through the Lord's Prayer

• DANIEL E. PAAVOLA •

CONCORDIA PUBLISHING HOUSE • SAINT LOUIS

Published by Concordia Publishing House
3558 S. Jefferson Ave., St. Louis, MO 63118-3968
1-800-325-3040 · cph.org

Copyright © 2017 Daniel E. Paavola

All rights reserved. No part of this publication may be reproduced, stored in a retrieval system, or transmitted, in any form or by any means, electronic, mechanical, photocopying, recording, or otherwise, without the prior written permission of Concordia Publishing House.

Scripture quotations are from the ESV® Bible (The Holy Bible, English Standard Version®), copyright © 2001 by Crossway, a publishing ministry of Good News Publishers. Used by permission. All rights reserved.

The quotations from the Lutheran Confessions in this publication are from *Concordia: The Lutheran Confessions*, second edition; edited by Paul McCain et al., copyright © 2006 Concordia Publishing House. All rights reserved.

Quotations marked LW are from Luther's Works, American Edition (56 vols.; St. Louis: Concordia Publishing House and Philadelphia: Fortress Press, 1955–86).

Text with the abbreviation *LSB* is from *Lutheran Service Book*, copyright © 2006 Concordia Publishing House. All rights reserved.

Manufactured in the United States of America

Library of Congress Cataloging-in-Publication Data

Names: Paavola, Daniel E., author.
Title: Our way home : a journey through the Lord's Prayer / Daniel E. Paavola.
Description: St. Louis : Concordia Publishing House, 2017.
Identifiers: LCCN 2016041662 (print) | LCCN 2016057355 (ebook) | ISBN
    9780758654786 | ISBN 9780758654793
Subjects: LCSH: Lord's prayer.
Classification: LCC BV230 .P225 2017 (print) | LCC BV230 (ebook) | DDC
    226.9/606--dc23
LC record available at https://lccn.loc.gov/2016041662

Matthew 6:9–13—The Lord's Prayer

Pray then like this:

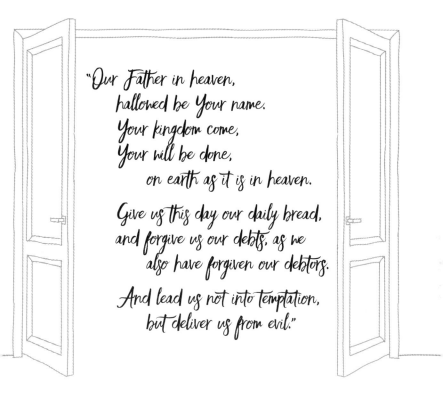

"Our Father in heaven,
    hallowed be Your name.
Your kingdom come,
Your will be done,
        on earth as it is in heaven.

Give us this day our daily bread,
and forgive us our debts, as we
        also have forgiven our debtors.

And lead us not into temptation,
    but deliver us from evil."

Anatomy of the Lord's Prayer

The Introduction:
Our Father
who art in heaven,

The Conclusion:
For Thine is the kingdom
and the power and the glory
forever and ever.
Amen.

The First Petition:
hallowed be
Thy name,

The Second Petition:
Thy kingdom come,

The Seventh Petition:
but deliver
us from evil.

The Third Petition:
Thy will be done on
earth as it is in heaven;

The Sixth Petition:
and lead us not
into temptation,

The Fourth Petition:
give us this day
our daily bread;

The Fifth Petition:
and forgive us our trespasses
as we forgive those who
trespass against us;

Contents

ACKNOWLEDGMENTS

HOW DO YOU SAY SOMETHING NEW ABOUT THE LORD'S PRAYER TO THOSE WHO HAVE KNOWN IT ALL THEIR LIVES? How do you teach it to lifelong Christians and, at the same time, to those who are new to the Bible and prayer? Those are the challenges that began my thinking of the Lord's Prayer as a journey. I first wrote about this concept in Butternut, Wisconsin, where I was pastor of St. Paul Lutheran Church from 1984 to 1996. Twice each year we had new adult member classes for adults who wished to join our church. Often the classes were a mix of lifelong Lutherans along with their spouses or spouses-to-be who were joining the church. So the challenge was this: how do you teach the Lord's Prayer and not bore those who have prayed it thousands of times, and at the same time not lose those who have rarely or never said the prayer at all? So I developed the idea of the Lord's Prayer as a journey as a fresh idea for mature Christians yet still easily grasped by those new to the faith.

Over the years, this idea of the Lord's Prayer as a journey has been refined by my students at Concordia University Wisconsin who have listened to my brief summary in New Testament and Bible classes. Many in class and also those attending retreats and conferences have refined the images of the journey and contributed their own ideas. Each of them has made the journey clearer.

Thanks for this understanding of the Lord's Prayer begins with my wife, Holly, and our three children, Christy, Steve, and Nicole. When the children were still living at home, we prayed together at night after supper, each child contributing a phrase, sometimes one as simple as "Dear Jesus, thank You for life." Our shared prayers shaped the image of a home, with a light that was always on, reflecting the certainty that our caring Father heard us. Thank you especially to Holly, who has shared these prayers and has seen the many answers that have come by prayer. My parents, Edwin and Linda Paavola, also formed that picture of the home with the light always on and a house that prayed. Thanks also go to the people of Butternut, Wisconsin, who patiently helped build this expression of the prayer. Finally, thank you to my students and colleagues at Concordia University Wisconsin for sharing the vision of the prayer that takes us home.

I hope that as you read, you are able to use your own experiences to illustrate the Lord's Prayer as a light that draws us home. Blessings to you as you hear the promises of God to hear us when we pray. I trust that you will be drawn to our heavenly home by the timeless words of the Lord's Prayer.

{ I'm Going Home }

NEXT TO THE WORDS "I LOVE YOU," THE WORDS "I'M GOING HOME" MIGHT BE WARMEST WORDS WE EVER SAY. These words calm us or they exhilarate us. They're the force by which we move mountains, and they're our consolation when mountains fall on us. "I'm going home" is either our contented sigh or our determined vow.

These words also comfort us. As a child, you cried, "I'm going home," when you skinned your knee. Later in life, no matter what had happened, the door to home was always open for you. You were safe once you got inside. I hope it's still the same for you today. Your home—whether your childhood home or the home in which you now live—is ready to take you in. As you enter on a dark night, you don't need the lights. The floor creaks exactly where you know it will. The banister is smooth where you've rubbed it a thousand times. Your old chair welcomes you and never asks where you've been. You say, "I'm going home," because home takes you in.

These words also energize us. "Tomorrow, I'm going home" is a thought that keeps you up all night. In the morning, you pack in a rush and toss your bags and clothes into the car. Who cares how you look! You're going home. You jingle your car keys on your way to the driver's door just to hear the sound that rings out, "I'm going home!" People approach you as you open the car door, but you call out, "Sorry! Can't talk. I'm going home!" You start the engine and put the car in *We may not know every detail of heaven's blueprint, but we know that our Father is there.* drive. You count every mile as better than the one before because every mile brings you closer to home.

"I'm going home" is also the consolation of our prayer. The Lord's Prayer shows us heaven as our Father's home. He has brought us to His home in His Son, and our prayers remind us that our Father hears us in heaven. Our Father's home is our solace when we're battered. We pray as tired children who need the reassurance that our voices are already heard in heaven. Our Father welcomes us as children who've come a long way and who need the reassurance that our home with Him is ready. In His kingdom, He remembers us and draws us to Himself.

This home is also our excitement. We're children running for home when we pray. We may not know every detail of heaven's blueprint, but we know that our Father is there. We pray because of His command and also because, astonishingly, our Father hears us in heaven. Prayer reminds us that the home we have never seen is being filled with our voices every time we pray. Our words break into the heavenly court, and we enter His presence at that very moment. As distant as heaven seems from us today, we don't have to wait a lifetime for our voices to come alongside our Father. "I'm going home" isn't a distant, "someday" hope. It is the electric truth that powers our prayer as we pray, "Our Father . . ."

Heaven Is Our Home . . . So Let's Go Home!

The connection prayer gives us with our heavenly home is a bit like a child coming home from his or her new school in a new city to a brand new house. Several years ago, in late August, my wife and I and our three children moved to the small town of Cedar Grove, Wisconsin. The first Monday after our move, our children started their new school. While waiting to close on our house, we were living in a nearby hotel. When someone asked our children where they lived, they didn't say, "The Super Eight," even though that was technically true. Rather, they said, "The gray house by the library." It was a house they had barely seen, had walked through

While we come closer to home, His Son walks with us and assures us that we will end this journey with Him, surrounded by His kingdom, power, and glory.

once, and wouldn't live in for another five days. But to them, that gray house was home. Finally, on Friday, they got to come home to their new, real home. Not one child asked to go back to the motel. For the first time, they could say, "Let's go home."

We're all living on earth as a temporary motel for however many years God grants us. We depend on the promises of our Father about heaven, this home we haven't yet seen. In the meantime, we reach it in our prayers. The Lord's Prayer assures us that we are part of the company of heaven, with all those who stand before our Father. When we pray, we are eager children running down the road to home. Best of all, we know that our voices have already gotten there. We haven't actually crossed the threshold yet, but we see our Father before us and we know He hears us as we're coming. While we come closer to home, His Son walks with us and assures us that we will end this journey with Him, surrounded by His kingdom, power, and glory.

An Overview

In this Introduction, we see prayer as this remarkable opportunity that God offers His children. Prayer gives us more responsibility and adventure than we ever would have imagined. Following this look at prayer's opportunity, we see the overall journey that the Lord's Prayer makes. We begin with our Father in heaven, walk with Him on earth, and call for Him to lift us safely back to heaven again. This journey through the Lord's Prayer is like our daily commute—a drive that is the same, yet changing each day. After exploring this comparison, this chapter introduces three goals for the entire book: (1) the unity of the prayer as a journey, (2) the nearness of God to His children in each step, and (3) the beauty of each petition as a part of our trip with our Father on our way home.

Thy versus You

It's important to use the right title for the right person. Doctors like to be called "Doctor" and professors like to be called "Professor." So when we speak to God in His prayer, we should get the title right. But it can be confusing. Should we say, "Our Father who art in heaven, hallowed be *Thy* name"? Or should we be a bit more contemporary and say "hallowed be *Your* name"? "Thy" is the traditional wording found in many church hymnals and reflects the King James Version translation of the Lord's Prayer. The second method, "Your," echoes contemporary Bible translations of the prayer and some more recent liturgies.

Is one of these right or wrong? I suggest that you follow suit with your congregation when in worship, saying either "Thy" or "Your" as the printed text directs. (Though, to make things interesting, you could be like some of my former congregation members who, in their later years, would slip into the German of their youth when saying the Lord's Prayer.) The formality of "Thy" and "Thine" gives a respectful tone to the prayer, and you can certainly prefer that. However, in the end, God knows what we are saying and our desire to honor Him.

In this book, you will note that I use both "Thy" and "Your." When discussing the original biblical text of the prayer found in Matthew and Luke, I use "You" and "Your" as this is most likely the translation you find in your Bible if it is a recent translation, such as the ESV or NIV. When speaking of our formal use of the prayer in worship, "Thy" and "Thine" are used most often. In either case, we do our best to translate the Bible's words well into modern language while also valuing the historic, liturgical use that has been loved for centuries.

You Don't Have to Wait Any Longer

Remember some of the things you wanted to do when you were growing up, but you were told that you were too little? You were too young to cross the street by yourself. You weren't responsible enough to care for a puppy. You couldn't get a bike, couldn't get your ears pierced, and weren't taken seriously when you said you were in love. Our first twenty years are a song whose refrain could be, "Not yet. Too young. Someday. Just wait, just wait, just wait."

Imagine that your parents surprise you in the middle of that unending refrain. They walk you to the big front window of the pet store, point to a puppy, and say, "Wouldn't you like to take care of him? We know you'll do a great job." Next, when you're a little bit older, your parents buy you the tent you've been asking for forever and let you set it up for some backyard camping. You're perfectly safe there and yet, what an adventure. Then when you're sixteen, they toss you the keys to the car and say, "Take it out for a ride." I wonder if we'd believe them. These are all dreams come true. There has to be a catch. But if our parents keep insisting, we might just take the puppy, get in the tent, and drive the car.

As impossible as this sounds, I believe God acts even more astonishingly with us when He invites us to pray. We're children who see dimly and know only in part, as Paul says in 1 Corinthians 13:12. We could expect that God would want such children to be merely seen and never heard. After all, what can we add to the chorus of unending praise in heaven? What do we know of the will of God, and who are we to suggest what He should do? Besides mumbling poorly our confessions and our thanks, who are we even to approach God?

But He tosses us the keys and says, "Take a drive. Take in heaven, earth, and heaven again. Call to Me in heaven. Remember the needs of earth, but then come back to heaven again." He gives us a glimpse of His entire world and says, "Here, ask for what's needed." He allows us to camp here on earth, far from our heavenly home, but He leaves us a way to call Him when the night turns too dark for us. He actually entrusts us with the keys to His court and says, "Come any time. Stay as long as you like."

If our parents had actually given us the puppy, the tent, and the car keys, I imagine we'd be torn between actually believing them and saying, "Are you serious?" We feel the same way when we hear the actual promises of prayer. Prayer stands on the astonishing words of Matthew 7:7, "Ask, and it will be given to you; seek, and you will find; knock, and it will be opened to you." If this were some ordinary door and any plain request, it would be no surprise. We're used to easy offers of great gifts that later turn small—like restaurant chains that entice us with million-dollar prizes but give us only free fries. But with prayer, we're confronted with the door to the court of heaven. This is the door which we're promised will open when we call upon our Father in heaven. He promises, basically, "Call Me, even in the realms of heaven, and I will hear you and open that door." Do we dare to knock on that door and expect it to open for us?

This sort of audacious action is the essence of the Lord's Prayer. In fact, the image of daring words spoken in front of a closed door is the context of the Lord's Prayer. After the Lord's Prayer in Luke 11, the immediate following context in verses 5–8 is the parable of the friend at midnight. Only Luke records this parable, which is at first a bit unusual as an encouragement for us to pray. It tells of a man who comes to his friend at midnight, asking for bread for a traveler who has just arrived. The friend inside says he cannot get up, open the door, and give any bread. Yet in verse eight, the friend does get up—though not because he is a kind friend, but because he wants the friend to go away and leave him alone. Shameless impudence, not the kindness of friendship, opens the door.

We might anticipate that following the prayer in which we call God our Father we would have a parable stressing our own friendship with God or our status as the adopted children of God. The parable in Luke, however, gives us hope of something better than the need to depend on being a good friend of God. If God answers us because of our friendship, corrosive doubt would soon ask, "How good a friend have you been?" If we were to answer honestly, we would slip quietly away without knocking, especially if mere friendship was the key that opened the door.

But this door on which we knock is opened by the bold belief that our Father would certainly honor the Son's promise in Matthew 7:7: "Ask, and it will be given to you; seek, and you will find; knock, and it will be opened to you." The word in Luke 11:8 translated as "impudence" is ἀναίδεια, *anaideia*, a Greek word that is used only this one time in the New Testament. It means persistence, boldness, and even shamelessness. God appears at times as a fixed door. But what appears to be a closed door only makes our prayers stronger. This same boldness allows us to use the very words given to the disciples so that we shamelessly slide into their place as followers of Jesus. Our prayer is the act of faith taking God at His full word. It pleases Him because we trust His words as true, even when they astonish us.

Imagine our earlier situations. Dad tosses the keys to you, the sixteen-year-old. If he really did, and if you really believed him, then you would smile, say thanks, slide behind the wheel, and roll down the driveway. If your parents really offered you the puppy, you would catch him up in your arms and start trying out names. You would call your friends after your parents bought the tent and convince them that you really are camping this weekend on your own. You wouldn't waste time waiting until you grew up some more. Take the keys, the puppy, and the camping trip. Your father offered them, and he meant it.

So with our prayers, our boldness opens the door. This matches the very situation of the Lord's Prayer, especially in Luke 11. The disciples ask Jesus to teach them to pray, presumably because they overheard Jesus or at least saw Him pray (v. 1). Imagine the confidence of that request. "We saw You speaking with Your Father. We want to do the same. Teach us to do what You were just doing."

Pray even when . . .

We're thankful that the Lord's Prayer gives us the exact words to say, but we still wrestle with our worries. How can I pray? Especially, how can I pray when I feel that my words and my worries are so insignificant? We wonder if we can pray when we have small lives and worried faith. Throughout the book, in the "Pray even when . . ." sidebars, we examine how we can pray even with our reservations. Wonderful biblical people reassure us that we can pray even when . . .

Pray even when
ALL YOU CAN ASK IS, "LORD, TEACH US TO PRAY" (LUKE 11:2).

Jesus' disciples voiced this essential request, which triggered Jesus' second account of the Lord's Prayer. What a welcome request, and one Jesus was glad to fill. Let this be our starting point also. Ask simply, "Teach me to pray." Here is a lifelong desire. Asking to learn to pray doesn't contradict your past prayers as useless. But we can be sure that there is more to prayer than we've grasped so far. Teach me, Lord, how to pray endlessly, boldly, thankfully, creatively, kindly. It is enough to say, "Teach me to pray."

How easy it would have been for Jesus to put them off. *You're only children, and failing ones at that. You can't possibly speak to the Father. Be content to listen. Besides, what do you have to say, and why should He listen?* In short, as we heard countless times as we grew up, "Wait until you've grown up."

But Jesus says without any apparent hesitation, "When you pray, say . . ." He allows us the same intimate address to God that He might use: "Father." He gives us words that stretch from heaven to earth.

We're invited to praise God when we deserve to say only confessions of our sins. We're given hope of eternal deliverance when we deserve only wrath. We're asking for bread and forgiveness without any doubt that they will be given. Celebrate the bold maturity that's given to us in the prayer. Take these keys to heaven's door and use them.

The Journey Is the Key

The idea of a young person setting out on his or her first trip in the car works not only for the boldness of prayer but also for illustrating prayer as a journey. The Lord's Prayer is an adventurous trip with God, following the path laid out by Jesus in the prayer. Central to this book is this sense of movement seen in the prayer's specific words and the organization of its petitions. Our analogy of a trip fits the Lord's Prayer, in which we travel from heaven to earth and back to heaven in a spatial sense. Before we look at the exact steps in the prayer, let's sense the feeling of movement in the text.

Matthew's version of the prayer, Matthew 6:9–13, is the primary text we will use. In those verses, the first description of God is as the Father in heaven, a distinction of both location and nature from us. This distinctiveness is repeated in the Third Petition with the phrase "on earth as it is in heaven." The two realms of heaven and earth are held in tension; they are not identical to each other, and yet they are united under God's action. We're invited to reach the Father though He is in heaven, and we ask God to place the pattern of heaven over our own earth.

In addition to the references to heaven and earth, the prayer also supports the pattern of a journey by some of the key verbs, which have a sense of movement. The Second Petition begins this movement with the common verb "come." We call on God as Father and King to bring His kingdom to earth as a moving force. Later, in the Sixth and Seventh Petitions, there are the verbs "lead us not" and "deliver." These both have a balancing idea with the earlier "come." While we ask that the kingdom of God would come nearer, we also ask that we would be taken away from danger and the realm of evil. God brings His kingdom nearer and at the same time draws His children farther from their enemies.

Another aspect of this balance between the opening and closing petitions is found in the pronouns used throughout the prayer. Each of the first three petitions refers to God by the second person singular pronoun, "You." After this, it is not used again, except for the traditional ending employed by many denominations, "For Yours is the kingdom and the power and the glory forever. Amen."[1] Then, starting in the Fourth Petition, the pronouns put the focus on our needs, our bread, our debts, our debtors, and our deliverance from evil and temptation. A simple structural understanding might say that we pray first for the things of God in petitions one through three and then pray for ourselves in petitions four through seven.

However, this division might lead some to separate the prayer into a heavenly half and an earthly half. Yet, the prayer has a unity through all the petitions. God is just as near in petitions four through seven as He is in the first three. His leading and rescuing take us from a multifaceted evil and deliver us to the single, saving Father. We understand that we are fed, forgiven, led, and rescued by and for Him. We begin with the Father, addressed and praised, and end with His works, which are all around us. The desire for His kingdom to come and His will to be done is the gateway for the following petitions of bread and forgiveness. It is possible to see the relationship between the Second and Third Petitions and the last four in this way: in the Second and Third Petitions we pray, "Your kingdom come, Your will be done on earth as it is in heaven," declaring that in God's kingdom and will is everything He will do for us. He will bring us our daily bread, forgive our sins, see us forgive others, lead us, and deliver us. Then, in the final four petitions, we are intimately wrapped with the fulfillment of our earlier desire for His name, kingdom, and will.

Therefore, the Lord's Prayer begins with the Father in a distinct, yet approachable heaven. We are boldly invited to His door and taken up with the wonders of His kingdom. However, we can't remain there but are drawn back to the concerns immediately around us. We invite His kingdom, gifts, direction, and deliverance here so that we may permanently ascend to His kingdom.

1 This ending is generally not printed in modern translations of the text, but is included in a footnote. This is the case with the English Standard Version, the New International Version, the Revised Standard Version, and the New Revised Standard Version. The New American Standard Version places it in the text within brackets, while the King James and New King James versions print it in the text without any distinguishing marks. The disagreement concerning these words revolves around their absence in many of the earliest manuscripts of the New Testament and their inconsistent rendering in some of the manuscripts that do include them. For example, some late Greek manuscripts expand the phrase this way: "for Thine is the kingdom and the power and the glory of the Father and of the Son and of the Holy Spirit forever. Amen."

A Brief Overlook of the Journey

Harrington Beach State Park in Belgium, Wisconsin, is along the shore of Lake Michigan. The beach is mostly sand with a few patches of small rocks. However, there is one stretch where the shore turns to solid rock, and when the lake level is just right, you can leap from rock to rock. At first glance, the rocks appear to be distinct and separate. But then you look deeper and see that they're actually one long, flat rock, a shelf of stone just below the water.

Maybe you've crossed a river or skirted a lakeshore, leaping from rock to rock. Every slippery stone lies separate from the others, each threatening to be the one that will slide out from under you. But at Harrington Beach, it's all one solid stone. You don't have to worry. That rock's not going anywhere, no matter how much weight you put on it. You might not see the connection between each step. But the stone holds fast because it is all one rock.

The Lord's Prayer is that solid stone. The petitions might look like separate pieces with little connection to one another. But they're all of one stone, connected below the surface of our first glance. It's the Lord's Prayer, the Lord's own thought, and the Lord's own journey from heaven to earth and heaven again. The certainty of the journey is not determined by our careful balance or our choice of the right rocks and steps. The prayer is itself an unbroken, solid path that cannot slip out from under us. Tentative steps are not necessary, hoping the rock stays under us. We can stride through each petition confidently, from one absolute and secure stone to the next. Each step is a solid stride to the final end in heaven.

The prayer's journey is a long path, one that begins in heaven with the opening words of the Introduction, "Our Father who art in heaven." This puts us with the Father in the highest realm. Then, the First Petition remains on this level, praising God with the saints and angels, "hallowed be Thy name." On our diagram, we begin in the upper left with our Father in heaven and praise Him with the choir of heaven. The Second and Third Petitions then transition downward. Imagine the path or line that represents the journey as beginning an angled, almost reluctant stepping downward that matches the phrases, "Thy kingdom come, Thy will be done on earth as it is in heaven." As we pray, we invite the Father to do His work on earth as He has seen it done in heaven. It's our view of our Father in heaven that makes us ask for

His kingdom and His will to come to earth. The one who prays is like a child who asks her father to come with her to her room because it is too dark or she can't clean her room all on her own. And so she asks her father to come and make this room more like his own. This request is like our own transition between heaven and earth in the prayer. We want our Father to come with us to make our rooms reflect His perfect home.

Heaven pours out an extravagant waterfall of forgiving grace, so great that it overflows past the one who is forgiven.

HEAVEN

HEAVEN

OUR FATHER
—NAME

KINGDOM
& POWER

KINGDOM COME

DELIVER US

WILL BE DONE

LEAD US NOT

DAILY BREAD

FORGIVENESS

EARTH

After this transition toward earth, we now look up during the Fourth and Fifth Petitions, bread and forgiveness. Picture yourself firmly on earth but with a clear view upward. The gifts of the Fourth Petition come as a gentle shower, filling but not overwhelming the earth. God sends gifts of daily bread in His continuing protection of His children. The Fifth Petition, however, asks for a flood of forgiveness. Heaven pours out an extravagant waterfall of forgiving grace, so great that it overflows past the one who is forgiven. There is so much forgiveness that one cannot help but see it spread to those unforgiving trespassers who surround each of us.

> We step through troubled waters onto the absolutely sure rock of each petition raised up for us to follow and trust.

But don't be swept away. The analogy of a flood is helpful for the Sixth Petition and our plea that we not be swept into temptation. Here we're beginning our return in thought to heaven. We ache to be done with the dangers that surround us, and so we ask that we would be delivered from evil. Just as our path descended in the Second and Third Petitions, going from heaven to earth, here let it ascend back to the Father. With our asking "Thy kingdom come, Thy will be done," we ask our Father to come where we live and to straighten our lives according to His heavenly pattern. We end the prayer as children asking that He would finally lift us up out of this world and take us to Himself. That is the triumphant feeling of the traditional conclusion, "For Thine is the kingdom and the power and the glory forever and ever. Amen." Think of these words as the songs we sing and the steps we take as we ascend to Him.

That flow from heaven to earth and back to heaven again is the cohesive pattern for the Lord's Prayer, which this book unfolds. It gives the prayer a unity within each of its parts. The individual petitions build upon one another as steps in a journey. They introduce the scenes and suggest the people and other beings we meet on this journey. We take in all of creation. We travel from the praising angels and saints who hallow God's name to the most troubling people in our lives, those who owe us an enormous debt. We are reminded of our own frailty but also of the mighty protection of our rescuing God. This journey allows us through the few words of the prayer to take in the broad sweep of God's creation and His works on our behalf. We step through troubled waters onto the absolutely sure rock of each petition raised up for us to follow and trust.

The Same Road Is Never the Same

The image of the prayer as a single stone ledge with steps formed from that same rock might suggest that it is an overly worn path. Aren't the petitions stones rubbed smooth by now? After all, we've traveled over this same path thousands of times. Yet, the beauty of a regular journey is that it balances the unexpectedly new with the comfortingly familiar. Think of the trips that you make over and over again, such as going to work, getting children to school, or going back home to your parents' house. You know the rhythm of every mile. You've named the potholes. You meet the same white car with the memorable bumper sticker in the same stretch of highway most every day. In many ways, this road never changes. It always starts and ends in the same places with the same turns along the way.

Yet, for all its familiarity, this road is never the same. Every day this journey is different. You don't have to take the same street. You can turn left, not right, and go the long way, the scenic route off the interstate. The weather is never the same day to day. As I write this, it is finally spring in Wisconsin. Today it's in the mid-seventies, with long grass and wildflowers along the roads. My motorcycle ride into work this morning was the first time I could smell warm fields and feel the coming heat of summer. On the other hand, that same stretch of road with winter blizzards, sleet, and forty-mile-an-hour winds gives you an adventure worth talking about when you get home.

The beauty of a regular journey is that it balances the unexpectedly new with the comfortingly familiar.

Those with whom you travel also change. Perhaps you carpool or take children to school. Their excitement or worries take center stage some days. The people in the vehicles next to you are a wonderful balance of the new and familiar. You've never seen someone driving and shaving at the same time before, but you did today. Your thoughts went to your childhood home today when you saw a semitruck from your hometown. Finally, your own vehicle brings life to these same miles. Your trusty Civic stumbles home with a stuck thermostat and the temperature gauge soaring—that's a trip you'll remember. The journey is never the same if we have the eyes to see the differences. And so praying the Lord's Prayer need never be the same because the world in which we pray changes, as do we, every day.

Let's Go Home a Different Way Today

The Lord's Prayer is a journey with this same balance of familiar and new. Like our commute, it has a prescribed start and end with its steps set by someone else. It is the *Lord's* Prayer since He established each petition, giving us a clear beginning and end. This is not our private, clueless wandering toward God. The prayer is a reminder of the One whose sacrifices made this trip possible in the first place. The Lord's Prayer is a return to the whole work of Christ for us. The prayer impresses us with the sense that we are traveling over the steps of the ultimate Pioneer. We walk among the words of the Lord's Prayer in awe of

When we pray, we follow in the furrow cut by His cross.

the One who dared to become flesh to journey with us. But He made the journey not as an impossible, solitary path but as the way that brings us to the Father. Repeating His words in prayer reminds us of the sacrifice that makes our journey to the Father possible. When we pray, we follow in the furrow cut by His cross.

Every word is fixed also by His intention of bringing us home. We use the mirrors of faith and His Word to look back on His walk. But our central focus is on what lies ahead. Your journey to and from work each day always gets you home. The Lord's Prayer, despite the interruptions of our wandering thoughts, brings us home relentlessly. We always begin with our heavenly Father and always end with the praise of His kingdom, power, and glory. But our worst sins can't stop this journey from bringing us to the forgiveness of the Fifth Petition. Our worst fears cannot stop us from being delivered and ascending to His kingdom, power, and glory. We begin with the Father, and He always sees us home by the end.

CROW THE SEED OF . . .

When he was just beginning to rule as king, Solomon wisely prayed for more wisdom (1 Kings 3:5–14). Wisdom was a seed already growing well within Solomon, but he knew he needed more to rule.

Throughout the Lord's Prayer, we can be reminded to ask for more of those things that we already have. Many of our prayers can be like Solomon's, asking that the seed, which we already have, would grow. In this set of sidebars, we are going to use Solomon as our model, seeing in Proverbs those qualities, such as wisdom, that are already with us as small seeds and that we hope to see grow. Wisdom wisely asks to increase in the fear and awe of God. So we start by asking with Solomon, "Give your servant therefore an understanding mind" (1 Kings 3:9).

Yet, for all of its constancy, the Lord's Prayer takes us on a new journey each day. You can likely choose several routes for your daily commute. Going to work, I can take the interstate almost the whole way, or I can ride the two-lane back roads and kick up dust on dirt roads. Like your choice of roads, there is a choice of paths within the Lord's Prayer. We have different accounts of the Lord's Prayer in Matthew 6:9–13 and Luke 11:2–4. Matthew's account is the one traditionally used in worship and is likely the most common in private prayer. Luke's version is strikingly shorter, beginning with only "Father," omitting the Third Petition, "Your kingdom come . . . ," rephrasing slightly the request for forgiveness by speaking of sins rather than debts, and omitting the last petition, "deliver us from evil." The version in Luke may be compared to the road home that, though it is shorter in actual miles, really takes you a bit longer to travel due to traffic. Luke's version of the prayer slows us as we pray, making us unexpectedly stop and omit words that we have already begun to say. We are reminded by these changes in Luke's text of the essential core of the prayer whereby we begin with the Father, praise Him, yearn for His kingdom, find His work in our food and forgiveness, and like children with uplifted arms, ask to be taken up again from our surrounding temptations. The journey ends the same as in Matthew with praise of the Father's home. In Matthew and Luke's versions of the prayer, we are on parallel, but not identical, streets as we travel.

But even with the familiar words of the Lord's Prayer, we find that there is a rhythm of change in each day's saying of the prayer. The differences in the world around us change how we pray these words. We continually read about increasing violence in the Middle East, mudslides in California, earthquakes in Japan, hurricanes, fires, floods . . . All of these are the coloring behind our prayer, "Thy kingdom come, Thy will be done on earth as it is in heaven." We are praying that His hands shape a constantly changing world, a clay globe that never stops spinning on His potter's wheel.

That's change in the largest sense. These are the worries you share with millions of others. But there are more immediate changes possible. The people in your family probably motivate your prayers more than any ten million in the next state over. Your prayer, "Forgive us our trespasses as we forgive those who trespass against us," is more pointed today when your home is heavy with that unmistakable tension of unforgiven sins. "Give us this day our daily bread," rings more fervently when your health insurance writes that they will not cover your latest bill. Each day the people closest in our lives hold up a different facet of the prayer, revealing a shade of its light we've never seen before. It is not the same prayer as yesterday when we place it over the constantly changing people around us.

Finally, it comes down to you. Every day you drive the same miles, but some days, in a peaceful trance, you almost miss your exit, astonished that you're already there. Other days, you're a candidate for road rage, frustrated over every second lost in a drive that is taking forever. The road hasn't changed, but you certainly have.

We pray the Lord's Prayer with these same differences. One day, we linger on the First Petition, content to hallow His name while we wonder what the glory of heaven will be. We might never get beyond this first step of praise. The next day we feel the quicksand of temptation and our failure around us. We race over the stones of the early petitions in order to pray as soon as we can, "Forgive us our trespasses." But when we face the same trials tomorrow, we run ahead to the solid rock of asking, "Lead us not into temptation, but deliver us from evil." Each day gives a new tone to our prayer.

This individualism of our prayers allows us to take tangents within the saying of the Lord's Prayer. The prayer invites us to linger on each petition as we need. I've found it interesting to see how my wandering in thought from one petition leads me to other points in the prayer. This is the beauty of a familiar journey. You may drive along the road deep in thought and only ten miles later realize where you are. But, since you've taken this same trip every day, there's no danger of being lost.

In the same way, pray the Lord's Prayer as an everyday drive. You can take a sharp turn on any petition, tour the neighborhood of daily bread or things needing forgiveness, and then return back to the prayer. The prayer is a street always open, always ready to be traveled.

The pattern of the Lord's Prayer that I suggest in this book doesn't demand an immediate or rigid following of each petition after the other. While each petition has a place within the whole, each is poised to lead you ahead or back in thought to the neighboring petitions. This journey is short enough that at any point you can pause, look

The prayer as a journey is, therefore, a wonderful tension between the constant and the changing, the road that is perfectly known and the one promising something new around the bend.

forward or back, or take in the whole length. As I pray that His name be hallowed, I can do this because I can see His promise of forgiveness coming in the Fifth Petition. When I ask that He deliver me from evil, I am remembering again the glory of His name and heaven itself where my prayer began. I am praying to be delivered to the glory that began the prayer and which I can still see. The prayer as a journey is, therefore, a wonderful tension between the constant and the changing, the road that is perfectly known and the one promising something new around the bend.

It's the Trip That Counts

My idea of a vacation is a little strange. Fishing, Disney World, or a cruise? None of these are really me. I love the road. For eight years while I was in high school and college, I took a motorcycle trip as my summer break from school and farming. I rode as far as I could every day, often riding extra miles just to reach a milestone of 500, 600, and even 1,000 miles in a day. I rode to get somewhere beautiful like Colorado, the Great Smoky Mountains, or Yellowstone. But the excitement of the trip was getting up each morning with an entire day to spend riding down a road I'd never seen before.

I know that not everyone loves putting miles on the road. Maybe you want the shortest road possible to the resort or to the home of old friends. You don't want to load a new address in your GPS but instead just follow the familiar landmarks. I understand that love of the familiar and the warmth of the same place. I was always glad to get home from my trips for the same reasons.

In the Lord's Prayer, we have the excitement of the untraveled road along with the comfort of meeting those we love. The prayer is both adventure and reunion. We travel through the prayer so that we can discover how our Father will go with us today, in a way different from any other day. Pray the prayer right now, and it will be a different journey than ever before. You, your family, and the world all have needs that you didn't know of yesterday. You have reasons for thanks, glimpses of heaven's glory, and sins needing forgiveness that are different from yesterday.

Our Father who art in heaven,
hallowed be Thy name,
Thy kingdom come,
Thy will be done
   on earth as it is in heaven;
give us this day our daily bread;
and forgive us our trespasses

as we forgive those who
trespass against us;

and lead us not into temptation,
but deliver us from evil.

For Thine is the kingdom and the power
and the glory forever and ever. Amen.

In that newness is also the familiar sound of the Son's words addressed to the Father. We're on this journey with the Son, who guides us on His own heavenly tour. The words of the prayer reassure us that He'll bring us home. We become children when we pray the prayer—children who are first eagerly pressed to the window, looking ahead for something new, and later, children calmly leaning against our Father even when driving through a storm. We might recognize the newness of this day, or we might be blind to the dangers from which He is delivering us. But it doesn't matter. The Lord's Prayer delivers us home each time. We travel over these words each day to renew our relationship with our Father. Then we ask and look for what He is going to bring through this relationship. Whether facing the familiar or the frighteningly new, the Lord's Prayer is a journey that focuses on our Father and His bond with us.

Our Journey Together

The Lord's Prayer as this familiar, yet new, journey is our theme. Within that journey, there are three individual goals for the book. First, I hope it shows that the Lord's Prayer is united through each petition so that it leads you in a clear path. This view displays the beauty and planning of the prayer. The Lord's Prayer is far from a collection of random pieces that could be rearranged in any manner. It flows thoughtfully to bring us to the Father throughout His kingdom of heaven and earth. The interplay between heaven and earth allows each petition to build upon the past and to anticipate the petitions to come. In heaven, praise and prayer never cease, and so in the Lord's Prayer, we're drawn into the rushing flow of endless heavenly petitions that move between heaven and earth.

Second, the book should strengthen your sense of being immediately with God in prayer, reaching to heaven in the opening words and yearning for heaven at the close. We may often feel that we're only feeble-voiced children, stuck on earth, but here we dare to call from earth to heaven. As tiny as our voices are, we know that our Father hears us. This journey of the prayer begins in heaven with the Father's powerful arms sweeping us up. We may start prayer imagining ourselves to be abandoned children, alone in our own dark room, calling for a Father who is in His own distant place. But immediately upon beginning the Lord's Prayer, we realize that our voices and our very selves have already reached Him in heaven. We walk with Him throughout the whole prayer, through heaven and earth.

Third, this book should let us savor each step of the Lord's Prayer as a fitting stop in itself. While much of the focus is on the journey with its sense of movement, remember that each journey is a series of moments to be remembered. You don't film your entire vacation trip. You take pictures of each important moment. Later, you hold up one picture and spend an hour remembering that instant. The Lord's Prayer gives in each petition a fixed moment in our walk with our Father. Yes, each step tugs at our sleeves to move ahead to the next. But give yourself time to pause over each petition. Perhaps in your journey today you'll never get past the Fourth Petition and its rain shower of His gifts; you'll be too completely caught up in our Father's generosity to finish the journey in its entirety.

So we are on a journey with the One who loves us. The Lord's Prayer, with all its petitions, is a wonderful series of stops. But you don't need to apologize if today's conversation with the Father at one point was so long and loving that you made a new ending just for today. Tomorrow you'll start over again.

I hope that this journey is a daily walk for you with Him. The Father reaches us through these words. The words are a well-connected journey, but we don't need to hurry to the end. Savor each step. Together, may we discover our Father's way home.

CHAPTER ONE

{ Coming to Our Father's Home }

THE LIGHT WAS ALWAYS ON WHEN I CAME HOME. I grew up on a farm in western Minnesota with a white farmhouse at the end of a half-mile long gravel driveway. When I came home at night, my parents always had a light on in the kitchen. As soon as I turned onto the driveway, the light beckoned me, "Come on home."

I hope this image was true for you too. Mom or Dad (or both) was always up, waiting, and the lights were always on. But even better than that, our heavenly Father has greater lights burning for us. My parents' 100-watt kitchen light is a faint illumination compared to the searchlight coming from our Father's home. He draws all His children home every day through His invitation for us to pray. The words of the Lord's Prayer are a light that says our Father is always home, waiting to hear us come. And He will never fall asleep, unaware that we've come home.

In this opening chapter, we focus on the image of God as our Father and on our entry into His court through prayer. This starts our view of the prayer as a journey from heaven to earth and back to heaven again. We'll get a clear view of our Father through the lens of His Son. Our prayers are lifted up to the Father's home, and we're given the boldness to call Him "Our Father." When we see that we're with our heavenly Father, we can stop looking at ourselves in a mirror. The journey all starts when we see our Father in heaven by the light He has on.

No Pulling on the Necktie—No Hanging on the Window Shade

How do you see the action of prayer?

When you pray, where is God, and where are you?

When prayer connects you with God, who
moves to make the connection?

All these questions focus on the action of prayer. Let's define prayer as the communication between God and His people.[2] We have a combination of nearness and distance in this communication. On the one hand, God's presence everywhere means that He is perfectly near us. In fact, He is within us through the action of Baptism. He knows all our needs before we speak them (Matthew 6:8), and His Spirit prompts our prayer itself (Romans 8:26–27). Prayer recognizes the perfect knowledge and immediate presence of God. We reach our Father in heaven while never moving an inch on earth.

On the other hand, prayer transcends any tie to earth. Prayer deals with the most distant points imaginable. When we pray the Lord's Prayer, we're reminded that our Father dwells in heaven, while we do not. Certainly, heaven is not distinguished as a separated realm so that God is somehow restricted there, touching earth only by remote control.[3] However, the repetition of "in heaven" in the Introduction and in the Third Petition, "on earth as it is in heaven," reminds us that prayer joins two distinct realms, heaven and earth.

A vending machine immediately gives what you ask for, but nothing more; a Father always shows patience first.

Many people instinctively see prayer as this uniting activity. Prayer joins heaven and earth. We stand in the light reaching toward a distant sun. But we can get this prayer connection wrong. For many, prayer is like snatching upward, trying to get God's attention. He is heavenly distant, while we're bound to earth. Perhaps, when we pray, we need to pull God down to us.

2   Martin Luther defines our action in prayer this way: "Spiritual and sincere prayer reflects the heart's inner-most desires, its sighing and yearning." He stresses the value of brief prayer and the Lord's Prayer therefore as the certain, sure words given by God, both as God's word to us and our words to God, "for every absolution, all needs, all blessings, and all men's requirements for body and soul, for life here and beyond, are abundantly contained in that prayer" (LW 42:20, 22).

3   Martin Chemnitz defines heaven in a helpful way for the Lord's Prayer. It is the throne, seat, and abode of God where His glory, majesty, and power are seen. It is not a physically remote location, but the full exercise of His glory. Martin Chemnitz, *Ministry, Word, and Sacraments: An Enchiridion*, trans. Luther Poellot, J. A. O. Preus, and Georg Williams (St. Louis: Concordia, 2007), 29.

Imagine acting out this view of prayer. If God is in heaven and we're here, what do we have to do? How do we get His attention? Wave our arms? Tug on His necktie? Pull Him down like a window shade? We'll do whatever it takes to get God's attention and bring Him down to earth.

I suspect that we often see prayer in this way. Window-shade prayer is pulling God to earth to remind Him of our needs. There are some things here that need to change, and our prayer is pointing these out to God. We pull Him down like a window shade, show Him what's going wrong, and then snap Him back up to heaven, hoping things will change.

But what a sad image of prayer all this is. In this view, God is in heaven, but we're hopelessly here. He neither knows nor cares about what's happening. If we pursue this model of prayer, we'll spend our time clutching after a slippery God who wants to get away from us as fast as He can. He can't wait to rattle out of our hands and disappear past our reach.

We may even hear this attitude reflected in Psalm 10, which opens by asking the very questions of distance and ignorance that we wrongly attribute to God: "Why, O LORD, do You stand far away? Why do You hide yourself in times of trouble?" (v. 1) Because God seems distant even to the righteous, the wicked are easily convinced that God knows nothing of what goes on. Therefore, the wicked are bold in their destruction and vain in their rebellion against an invisible God: "In the pride of his face the wicked does not seek Him; all his thoughts are, 'There is no God'" (v. 4). In the following verses, the righteous see that the wicked are comfortable, haughty, and prosperous. The conclusion of the wicked seems inevitable: "He says in his heart, 'God has forgotten, He has hidden His face, He will never see it'" (v. 11). It's exactly this conclusion that drives necktie-pulling, window-shade prayer—the prayer of those who believe that God knows little of what goes on and does even less about the little He knows.

But this view of a distant Father should be only a brief eclipse in our thoughts. The psalmist cries against this idea of an empty-minded and weak-handed God in the closing verses of Psalm 10: "But You do see, for You note mischief and vexation, that You may take it into Your hands" (v. 14). God is the king over all the earth and the afflicted are heard (vv. 16–17). The one who prays is never forgotten. The psalmist adds a description of God that is most appropriate to our prayer: "O LORD, You hear the desire of the afflicted; You will strengthen their heart; You will incline Your ear" (v. 17). As Father, He knows our need, and He's ready to act.

Pray even when YOU'RE IN THE WRONG PLACE.

The Lord's Prayer lifts our words to the Father in heaven, but do we dare to pray? What if we're in the wrong place to start, a place that's as far from God in heaven as we can imagine? Take heart in Jonah 2 where Jonah, already in the great fish, prays, "When my life was fainting away, I remembered the LORD, and my prayer came to You, into Your holy temple" (v. 7). If Jonah, drowned under the judgment of God, can pray even in the belly of the great fish, you can pray even in your wrong place.

So we come to our Father in His light of heaven by way of the Lord's Prayer. Of course, the moments following our prayer may not bring immediate change. His action may not come at the instant His children demand. But His apparent delay is no reason to doubt His work as Father. Just as Hebrews 12:5–11 points out that discipline is evidence of our Father's relationship with us, so we might see His apparent slowness to answer as more proof of His Fatherhood. A vending machine immediately gives what you ask for, but nothing more; a Father always shows patience first, and then, later, He may also give that for which you ask.

Remember the light on at home when you turned up the driveway? Someone was waiting for you to come home. It's still true today with our Father in heaven. See the light of our Father's home. Don't be discouraged that cold and darkness still remain. Our Father knows what we need, and He sends first the light of His listening. That light might not immediately melt away our problems as we endure a frigid January snowstorm or a sweltering August heat wave, but His light in heaven is always on, always beckoning. He simply works in His own time. And it's when we begin the Lord's Prayer that we turn the corner on the road that leads to the Father's light.

A Hand Up

The light of God's care surrounds us even on cold days. Now imagine the actions that go along with our words of prayer. But don't draw God down to us like a window shade. If we don't pull Him down, what's left to bridge the distance? Let our Father be in heaven; join Him there through your words. Defy gravity and stand beside Him. That's the action of God in prayer.

When we call out, "Our Father who art in heaven," our Father brings us in word and thought into the very court of heaven. This is the light drawing us home. As we begin to pray, we name our Father by His location. But as the Father in heaven, He is not secluded in heaven, isolated from us on earth. Nor is He our Father who was formerly found in heaven but is now gone, having left that realm to listen to us. He is the Father who hears us in heaven. His gift of listening lifts us to join Him when we pray. His hearing elevates our thoughts to Him. This coming into His court isn't a rapturous, physical leaving of earth on our part; nor is it a mystical experience of unique emotions. Instead, the prayer's Introduction recognizes the truth that our Father, even while listening to us, is in heaven at that moment. Our words reach the heavenly court.

This way, "heaven" in our prayer reminds us of both the distant and near. While we call upon our Father, we're still firmly on earth. Frequently the New Testament presents heaven in contrast to our earthly existence. For example, the immediate context of Lord's Prayer in Matthew 6 speaks often of our heavenly Father who sees, provides, and rewards on earth even while He is clearly in heaven. Chapter 6 sets the tone of our Father who still affects earth while in heaven:

While Jesus distinguishes heaven and earth as distinct realms, He also shows the intimate connection between the two.

"Beware of practicing your righteousness before other people in order to be seen by them, for then you will have no reward from your Father who is in heaven" (v. 1). In the following verses, the Father sees charity

(v. 4) and prayer (v. 6) in secret and rewards them. Forgiveness given on earth corresponds with forgiveness given by the heavenly Father (v. 14). In verses 19–21, we're reminded to store up treasures in heaven, where our hearts will be. Verses 25–33 tell us to trust our heavenly Father, who knows our needs; to seek His kingdom and righteousness; and to receive from heaven our earthly needs. In Matthew 6, while Jesus distinguishes heaven and earth as distinct realms, He also shows the intimate connection between the two. As you act on earth, God sees and records all in heaven.

HEAVEN

HEAVEN

OUR FATHER
—NAME

KINGDOM
& POWER

KINGDOM COME

DELIVER US

WILL BE DONE

LEAD US NOT

DAILY BREAD

FORGIVENESS

EARTH

While Matthew 6 reminds us of the distinction between heaven and earth, other Scripture references to heaven speak of God's immediate presence around us.[4] Ephesians 1:20–23 recounts Jesus' ascension, so that the Father has "seated Him at His right hand in the heavenly places" (v. 20). There He dominates "above all rule and authority and power and dominion and above every name that is named" (v. 21). Ephesians 4:10 repeats this nearness of heaven, saying that Christ "ascended far above all the heavens, that He might fill all things." By His ascension, Christ is both near to the Father and simultaneously near to His Body, the Church. Our Father's heaven is not distant perfection; it is the immediate dwelling of the Trinity surrounding us.

The incarnation of Jesus, His putting on human flesh, provides a helpful model for our understanding of these two aspects of heaven's distance and nearness. In the incarnation, Jesus bridges the astonishing opposites of humanity and divinity, uniting the two into one person. Through the incarnation, all that can be said of both the human and the divine can be said of the person of Christ.[5] In the one Christ,

They questioned a sleeping carpenter and woke the mighty God.

we have the completely familiar—human flesh and bone—while at the same moment we have in our hands the eternal God. The disciples capture this wonder in the boat following Jesus' calming of the storm. They say, "Who then is this, that even wind and sea obey Him?" (Mark 4:41). They questioned a sleeping carpenter and woke the mighty God. Here is a man of an altogether divine power. It is the combination of

---

4   Albrecht Peters notes that Luther contrasted heaven and earth in the Third Petition, "O Father, Thou art in heaven, I your wretched child [am] on earth, in distress, far away from Thee . . ." However, heaven is not a physical barrier or entity. Peters defines Luther's understanding of heaven as "the dynamic center of divine omnipotence and omnipresence that escapes our spatially restricted conceptions" (Albrecht Peters, *Commentary on Luther's Catechisms: Lord's Prayer*, trans. Daniel Thies [St. Louis: Concordia, 2011], 5). Luther's explanation of the Second Article stresses the inclusion of believers with Christ in His ascension and dominion, "He has taken us as His own property under His shelter and protection [Psalm 61:3–4] so that He may govern us by His righteousness, wisdom, power, life, and blessedness" (Large Catechism, Part II, paragraph 30).

5   The Lutheran Confessions in the Formula of Concord, Solid Declaration, state, "In Christ two distinct natures exist and remain unchanged and unconfused in their natural essence and properties. Yet there is only one person consisting of both natures. Therefore, that which is an attribute of only one nature is attributed not to that nature alone, as separate. It is attributed to the entire person, who is at the same time God and man (whether the person is called God or man)" (Article VIII, paragraph 36). The Formula soon afterward quotes Luther, who picturesquely says, "Now if the old witch, Lady Reason, alloeosis' grandmother, should say that the Deity surely cannot suffer and die, then you must answer and say: That is true, but since the divinity and humanity are one person in Christ, the Scriptures ascribe to the divinity, because of this personal union, all that happens to the humanity and vice versa" (Article VII, paragraph 41).

His nearness and His divine difference that overwhelms them.

When we pray to our Father in heaven, we encounter this same combination. His divine difference from us is obvious in the very address of "Our Father in heaven." Heaven brings its appropriate images of the throne of God over all powers and creatures, as noted above in Ephesians. Yet, this heaven is not remotely (and perhaps comfortably) distant. In our prayer, we have recognized our Father's residence near us. He who is of heaven is here to listen to us. Even more, He brings us into His presence. Like the disciples in their familiar boat, we, in our familiar posture of prayer, stop in wonder when we recognize that we're in the presence of our heavenly Father. As they could stop to consider what they'd done in waking Jesus, we, in beginning our prayer, stand in awe at starting our conversation with our intimate, yet mighty God. The light we see comes from heaven itself and still reaches us at the very start of the prayer.

Finding Ourselves at Home

How are we going to dare to come into His heavenly home? If stepping into the heavenly court begins our journey, what makes us so daring as to come before the Father? While we may imagine that we're able to grasp God's necktie and draw Him to earth, isn't it even riskier to walk into His heavenly presence and speak as though He were waiting for us? To call from earth to a distant heavenly Father is one model of prayer. Even more dramatic is the real model, walking into the Father's own court.

In order to pray this boldly, we need three components:

a proper understanding of our Father

someone to bring us into His presence

and the very words to say

We begin with the wonder of a Father in heaven. I hope that our introductory words have amplified the grand act of prayer. We approach the glistening light of the Father's home. We might get a glimpse of heaven, but we'll never enter it if it's only a hall of perfect justice. Our sins will arrest us before we take one step. Neither will we enter heaven if it's only the spiritual battleground in which we rage "against the rulers, against the authorities, against the cosmic powers over this present darkness, against the spiritual forces of evil in the heavenly places" (Ephesians 6:12). Seeing conflict like that, we'll turn and run. We would be children at the end of the driveway who hear a battle raging at the house and decide now is not the time to go home.

But when we pray, we're not going to court or to battle. We're going home, our Father's home, in which there is no condemnation for those in Christ Jesus (Romans 8:1). Luther describes this freedom to pray as approaching our Father by His own invitation. In the Large Catechism, Luther writes, "For by this commandment God lets us plainly understand that He will not cast us away from Him or chase us away [Romans 11:1]. This is true even though we are sinners. But instead He draws us to Himself [John 6:44] so that we might humble ourselves before Him [1 Peter 5:6], bewail this misery and plight of ours, and pray for grace and help [Psalm 69:13]" (Part III, paragraph 11). The Lord opens the door to approach Him by portraying Himself as the Father.

As Father, God gives us at least two images that embolden our prayer. First, we see in God's fatherly creation a sure knowledge of ourselves. Psalm 103 builds a wonderful picture of God as a knowing and compassionate father: "As a father shows compassion to his children, so the LORD shows compassion to those who fear Him. For He knows our frame; He remembers that we are dust" (Psalm 103:13–14). Though He knows every detail of our sin, He doesn't act toward us on that basis: "He does not deal with us according to our sins, nor repay us according to our iniquities" (Psalm 103:10). We come to our Father, who knows exactly our limitations. Perhaps you came home to a parent who could tell from your first "Hi" that you had a miserable day. Instantly, my mom would say, "What's wrong?" If I asked, "How'd you know something's wrong?" Mom would reply, "I'm your mother. I can tell." Isn't it easier to tell our secret worries to someone who already knows them? So our heavenly Father invites us to come to Him, the one who already knows exactly what we have to say.

The second image of our Father, after Creator, is the Father who earnestly wishes the best for us. James 1:5–6 draws this picture: "If any of you lacks wisdom, let him ask God, who gives generously to all without reproach, and it will be given him. But let him ask in faith, with no doubting." Who doesn't lack wisdom? Our very lack of wisdom is often the motive to pray. However, we would be stopped in our first words if God were other than a Father. Remember James's promise. God gives to all generously and without reproach. We come to ask for direction. "Lord, what shall I do?" How easy it would be for God to respond immediately, "Why should I tell you? You haven't done what I've already told you. In fact, the trouble you have now is because you didn't listen to Me. I told you this would happen. Now figure your own way out."

That would be completely fair, but what father would meet his children this way? Our Father in heaven welcomes His children to come to Him even in the midst of the trouble that is their own fault. Jonah's cry in chapter 2 is an example of trust in this amazingly gracious God. Notice that Jonah acknowledges his guilt and the fact that God cast him into the sea: "For You cast me into the deep, into the heart of the seas" (2:3). Yet, he trusts that he can cry to this very same God, despite his wrongs. In verse 2, Jonah confidently says, "I called out to the LORD, out of my distress, and He answered me." He knows that he has a Father to whom he can come, even in the midst of being disciplined. The light from our Father draws us, regardless of the hour or what we've done.

The Father of One, and So the Father of All

Despite these assurances, our confidence in the light likely needs even more reassurance. Children don't run to a stranger and call him "Dad!" We don't drive up a lighted driveway just because it looks inviting. We have to know the homeowner before we go in. So who's going to bring us to a Father who is as distant as heaven?

The opening of the Lord's Prayer reminds us of that question. Once we have a glimpse of our Father and His light, we need someone to bring us into His presence. We need an introduction that allows us to say, "Our Father." Merely being created children of God or being part of the whole created world isn't enough. We can feel our need for a Father, but our emptiness isn't enough for us to call Him "Our Father." A child without a welcoming home needs a meal and a room. But just wanting a family and a home doesn't let the child open the door and sit down for supper. Someone needs to open the door.

The Son brings us home. He leads us, introduces us, and speaks for us to the Father. He flings open the Father's door and pours out heaven's light to draw us in. He even graciously shares His title "Beloved" with us so that, with Christ, we can dare to say, "Our Father."

First John 3:1 says, "See what kind of love the Father has given to us, that we should be called children of God; and so we are." In view of the only One who can rightly call out in prayer, "Father," we can come to our Father in His heavenly court. When we say, "Our Father," we stand before the Father with the true Son and count ourselves as part of the whole family of God. This fulfills the purpose of Jesus' coming, as John 1:12 says: "But to all who did receive Him, who believed in His name, He gave the right to become children of God."

Jesus Gives Us Our Father's Hand

When the Son brings us to the Father, He does it in word and deed, in at least three ways. First, He is the lens between the Father and us. Through Him, the Father sees us so that we really do appear as children, and likewise, through Christ, God appears as a Father to us. Second, He intercedes for us in the heavenly court so that our voices, in a tiny way, echo what He has already said for us. Third, Christ urges us forward before the Father. He both draws us from our frightened corner and gives us the words by which we can begin to pray. Jesus is the lens through which we see the world and heaven, and He stands beside us as we begin to speak to the Father.

Our two-word opening, "Our Father," is met with, "We were just talking about you."

So Christ is the lens through which we see God and God sees us. Ephesians 1:4 speaks of this: "He chose us in Him before the foundation of the world, that we should be holy and blameless before Him." God's knowledge of us before creation was through the only Son. His choice of us was completely conditioned through His love of His perfect Son. By seeing the Son, He saw us and therefore chose us. God is not shortsighted as to our sins. But He chooses to filter His vision, and so He focuses entirely on His Son when dealing with us.

To illustrate this, think of recording your children at a concert. Holly and I were some of the first parents in our children's school to have a camcorder back in the early 1990s. We recorded their concerts and Christmas programs and have miles of tape still today. Other parents asked if they could have a copy of the tape. Sure, glad to. But remember, I was taping *our* children. The tape was almost entirely focused on our children walking in, sitting, waiting to sing, and sitting again. Your daughter might have sung a beautiful solo, but I recorded our son sitting. When the program was over, all of us parents agreed it was a great performance. But each of us based our praise on what our child had done. Your daughter sang, our son sat. It's all good.

In a similar way, God chose us in view of His Son. His focus upon the world has always been through His Son's actions. His judgment upon each of us has been based on His Son. When He calls us His children, it is entirely in the likeness and view of His Son. First John 3:2 speaks of this: "Beloved, we are God's children now, and what we will be has not yet appeared; but we know that when He appears, we shall be like Him, because we shall see Him as He is." Colossians 3:3–4 carries the same image: "For you have died, and your life is hidden with Christ in God. When Christ who is your life appears, then you also will appear with Him in glory." It's true that we don't fully reflect God as perfect, mature children would. But now we are infants who only hint of the maturity we'll have one day.

Prayer isn't us trying to start a conversation. It's listening to the Father, Son, and Holy Spirit, who are already speaking of us, and joining in with what they've been saying.

Since we're not fully developed children, we're given the adopted state of beloved children (Ephesians 1:5). That is what we depend on when we cry, "Our Father." But our little voice is nothing compared to the One who is already speaking. Before we even approach God, Jesus, the perfect older Brother, is interceding for us. This is the second way He brings us before the Father. God knows all our needs before we ask Him, as Jesus makes clear in Matthew 6:8, saying, "Your Father knows what you need before you ask Him." Beyond this knowledge, however, the Son urges a compassionate hearing of our requests. Romans 8:34 is a powerful presentation of this scene: "Who is to condemn? Christ Jesus is the one who died—more than that, who was raised—who is at the right hand of God who indeed is interceding for us." Companion texts are Hebrews 7:25, "Consequently, He is able to save to the uttermost those who draw near to God through Him, since He always lives to make intercession for them," and Hebrews 9:24, "For Christ has entered, not into holy places made with hands, which are copies of the true things, but into heaven itself, now to appear in the presence of God on our behalf."

In the background of each of these texts is the death and resurrection of Christ. Romans 8:34 expresses the work of Jesus' death and resurrection through the contrasting question, "Who is to condemn?" Of all those who might condemn us in the heavenly court, no one is better qualified than Christ. He was tempted as we were (Hebrews 4:15) and yet never faltered. He bore the sins that we committed, but He never failed. He died because of what we did. If anyone could condemn us, He's the one. Given His death, would we ever dare to meet His Father? If we ever did come near to Him, the only question we should hear is, "Who killed My Son?" And our only prayer would be that He would never find us.

But that's not what the Father is saying in heaven. When we come to the heavenly court, we hear our own name. Before we say, "Our Father," we hear the Father and Son already talking about us. There's no sullen silence between the Father and Son and us. There's no need for an introduction. Our two-word opening, "Our Father," is met with, "We were just talking about you." What would they, the perfect Son and the almighty Father, say about us? Here Romans 8:34 rushes in to reassure us: "Who is to condemn? Christ Jesus is the one who died—more than that, who was raised—who is at the right hand of God who indeed is interceding for us." Jesus intercedes for you, for me, for everyone. The verb in Romans 8:34 for "intercede" is ἐντυγχάνω, *entunchano*. While this verb can mean simply, "to meet, to approach," here it has a stronger idea of intercession. The same word is used in 8:26–27 to describe the Spirit's intercession for us in groans too deep for words. Both the Spirit and the Son surround the Father's throne with appeals for us before we have begun the first syllable of "Our Father."

This is the sound that goes with the light that has drawn us all along. We come to the Father's home for the light, but as we get to the door, we hear our own name. Here, it's good news. The Father, Son, and Spirit are all speaking of us and for us. It's a conversation of forgiveness, love, hope, and joy. Listen, just listen. They're talking about you and it's all good. You can come through the door, no fears. Prayer isn't an awkward beginning. Prayer isn't us trying to start a conversation. It's listening to the Father, Son, and Holy Spirit, who are already speaking of us, and joining in with what they've been saying. Contemporary theologian John Kleinig, of the Lutheran Church of Australia, sums this up well: "When we pray, we engage with the three persons of the Holy Trinity. We pray to the Father; we pray together with the Son; and we pray by the power of the Holy Spirit. What we do when we pray depends entirely on what the Son gives us in His Word and on what the Spirit does with us through our faith in Christ."[6]

In a way, then, our beginning in the Lord's Prayer is already the ending. In one sense, there's nothing more to say. We can call God "our Father" and overhear the Father and Son talk about us. Just stand there and be stunned by the Son's passionate appeal. What's left to say except "Thank You" and "Amen"? Isn't this the complete opposite of that opening idea of prayer, the tugging on God's necktie, pulling Him down like a window shade? There's no distant God here, no need to tell Him what He seems to have forgotten. Our Father knows us, loves us, and has prepared all things needed for us, all of which comes by His Son.

It's like the time you stumbled upon your parents wrapping your Christmas gifts. You were coming to them with your wish list. But before you said a word, before you came around the corner, you heard their voices, and you heard your name. They were talking about all they had already bought for you. You put your list away and don't say a word. You listen for a minute and then go back to your room. You go to sleep to the happy sounds of paper, scissors, tape, and your name. So we come to the Father's home, ready with our list. But we're stopped by all that He is already saying and doing for us. When you say, "Our Father who art in heaven," pause at His door, hear the voices already speaking about you, and listen to the gifts being wrapped.

GROW THE SEED OF GENEROSITY

"One gives freely, yet grows all the richer; another withholds what he should give, and only suffers want" (Proverbs 11:24). Coming into the Father's presence gives us a glimpse of His riches

6   John Kleinig, *Grace Upon Grace: Spirituality for Today* (St. Louis: Concordia, 2008), 167.

and His generous hand, which feeds and guards the world. Heaven is the full garden of the generosity of God. We have the seed, the beginning of the same generosity. We'll never match the riches of heaven's court, but a glance at His riches and power assure us that His promise is true: "Give, and it will be given to you. Good measure, pressed down, shaken together, running over, will be put into your lap" (Luke 6:38). Lord, let the seed of generosity grow in my life.

The Gift of Words to Say

So we could be done before we get started. That's true. But since we're here in the Father's house, we should say something. But what's there to say? We have already seen the first two actions of the Son for us in prayer. Christ has been the lens through which we see the Father. Also, we've known of His words spoken already on our behalf. Besides these two actions, He gives us even more. One of God's great gifts is the wording of the Lord's Prayer. These words may seem somewhat unnecessary since the Son is speaking for us already. After all, having said, "Our Father who art in heaven," we could just say, "Thanks," in the deepest way possible.

How do we say thank You in a truly meaningful way? Praise God we have the words that Jesus gives, the words that come preapproved by God. Luther understands this in the following way:

> This ‹the Lord's Prayer› is a great advantage indeed
> over all other prayers that we might compose ourselves.
> For in our own prayers the conscience would ever be
> in doubt and say, "I have prayed, but who knows if
> it pleases Him or whether I have hit upon the right
> proportions and form?" Therefore, there is no nobler
> prayer to be found upon earth than the Lord's Prayer.
> We pray it daily [Matthew 6:11], because it has this excel-
> lent testimony, that God loves to hear it. We ought not
> to surrender this for all the riches of the world. (Large
> Catechism, Part III, paragraph 23)

Perhaps someone will object that the Lord's Prayer is lacking excitement because it's the same old words. Everyone uses them, and we'll never stand out to God if that's all we say. But this all misses the awesome setting of God's court, where our prayers are heard. To insist on using our own words is to return to a necktie-tugging view of prayer—we're trying to snatch a moment of God's attention with fresher words than anyone else.

But in reality, we pray in the Almighty's court where our elder Brother has gone before. We're being heard among the saints and angels in all their perfection. We won't impress anyone with new words. Isn't it good to have the very words of Jesus with the promise that the Father is glad to hear them? Then, while we say the words of the prayer, Jesus stays beside us and behind us. He smooths out our stuttering and smiles over our asking. Hebrews 4:16 invites us to be bold in prayer: "Let us then with confidence draw near to the throne of grace, that we may receive mercy and find grace to help in time of need." Our confidence is founded in the work of Jesus, who has proven the trustworthy nature of His promises by accomplishing the unthinkable death and resurrection. Having carried the cross, He can be trusted to carry our prayers.

Having carried the cross, He can be trusted to carry our prayers.

So come home with confidence. Prayer is a balance of amazement and trust. Heaven is a light both dazzling and familiar. On one hand, we come with quiet steps, lingering near the entrance, stunned by the brilliance of our Father's throne. We say our opening words while our eyes are squinting in the light, barely able to take it in. On the other hand, we're coming home. We're drawn by His light, like the light from the kitchen window. We walk into the sound of our own name, spoken by our elder Brother. By everything He's done, we come home.

No Mirrors on Mountains

Having come home by these words, what do we see? In the next petitions of the prayer, we focus on God's kingdom, His earthly gifts, ourselves as forgiven sinners, and more. But before we see all that, let's take in the view from the court of heaven.

I have never seen mirrors on mountaintops. Drive up a Rocky Mountain road to a ten-thousand-foot pass and stop on the side of the road. Bare stone cliffs and green, misty valleys stretch out. You take deep breaths, fill your phone with pictures, and record a video of the eagle way over there. But have you ever seen a mirror on the mountain?

Imagine someone going all the way to the top of a mountain, only to look for a full-length mirror. Why would anyone look for a mirror on top of a mountain? Only to see himself, of course. But what a waste! You're on the top of the world. Surely there's something more important, more impressive to see than another glimpse of yourself. And yet how many of your prayers begin by looking for a mirror. Mirror prayers never see past you. Mirror prayers reach heaven only to admire and talk about you. Heaven itself and the Lord who fills it can't crowd into that little mirror. It's got just enough room for you.

But mountaintops help us see beyond ourselves. Mountains show us size and power we'll never see in ourselves. There's beauty beyond our tiny reflections. I think that beginning our prayer in the heavens with our Father brings us to the mountaintop of heaven itself. Our thoughts are drawn beyond our immediate needs. No mirrors, no posturing, no perfect grooming needed. Instead, look where you are! The Father's court certainly trumps any list you brought about me, myself, and I.

By praying with this overview of heaven, how much more we can say, "Our Father." Our prayer isn't through the narrow view of our own cracked mirror. We may have started to pray with a list of worries, but the list can wait. We've been taken to heaven and it's time to enjoy the view. Luther noted how distracted our prayers can be, and he contrasts these futile words with genuine prayer: "This is why I maintain that there is nothing more laughable that anyone could possibly come up with than watching how mixed up thoughts become when a cold, distracted heart produces them while you are praying. But now, God be praised, I realize what a poor prayer it is when one forgets even what one was praying! A true prayer meditates on all the words and thoughts of the prayer, from beginning to end."[7]

From this heavenly perspective, the three key words, "Our," "Father," and "heaven," capture our attention and become our experience. We find that we're not alone but surrounded by our fellow

7   Martin Luther, *A Simple Way to Pray*, trans. Matthew Harrison (St. Louis: Concordia, 2012), 14.

creation and ushered in by our heavenly Brother. Stunned by the view, we're here by the grace of our Father. The full measure of His creation and His mercy are expressed by listening to us in heaven. He's lifted our voices to the highest places. "Our Father who art in heaven" places us in the perfect place to begin our prayer.

And so the Father's light brings us home. There's light at the end of the driveway. And the voices there tell us we can come home. Our little words, by themselves, would never leave earth, but we've been heard by the Savior and placed before our Father. He has even shared with us His own words to say. Because of who Jesus is to the Father, we get to say, "Our Father who art in heaven." It's good to come home to the light.

CHAPTER TWO

{ Singing with the Heavenly Choir }

I CAN'T SING. AT LEAST, I CAN'T SING IN ANY WAY YOU'D WANT TO HEAR. I'm usually a half step flat, and I have all the rhythm of a man who just stubbed his toe. But that hasn't stopped me from singing and listening to music throughout the day. I especially like to sing as I ride my motorcycle. Inside my helmet, I think I sound pretty good, but thankfully, no one else can hear me.

When we begin the Lord's Prayer, we start to sing in harmony. At least, that's the prayer's intention. In the Introduction of the prayer, we began with "Our Father" and we recognized that we're not alone in saying this prayer. The Introduction brought us into the Father's heavenly home. We heard the reassuring words of the Father and the Son, welcoming us to pray. With the Introduction, we're set on the stage of the heavenly throne room. In this chapter, we further explore the wonder of prayer as harmonizing with the praise of the saints in glory, the angels in heaven, and all the saints on earth in prayer. We'll also examine the meaning of these opening words of the prayer, "Hallowed be Thy name," as expressions of the nature of God and His relationship with His people. We'll find in His name the majestic chords of our mutual song. This song lingers within us as our Father tunes our lives to Himself.

Passing the Choir Audition

I have never auditioned to sing in a choir. I've admired choirs and would have been glad to be a part of one, but I've never wanted to face the almost certain rejection that would follow my audition. A true nightmare would be finding myself mistakenly in the middle of a great choir that suddenly goes quiet, expectantly humming in the background, waiting for me to begin my solo. Of course, the director doesn't give me the pitch. I'm supposed to find that on my own. I can see the knotted brows of actually talented singers as they continue to hum, wondering how this impostor ever got in.

Now in the First Petition, we begin to pray in earnest as we say, "Hallowed be Thy name." This is like stepping forward into an already-singing choir, taking our part, and joining in. I hope that the thought of singing in the presence of God, the angels, and the saints in glory is daunting and even frightening for you. If you're like me and would never sing a solo on earth, what would possibly make you sing out in heaven? Wouldn't that be even more frightening than any concert solo or stadium anthem here? How are we to enter the heavenly ranks and harmonize with the angels' chorus? Who are we to speak, let alone sing, "hallowed be Thy name" with our faltering voices? Why should God gladly hear our words, no matter what we say? Shouldn't we rather be like Isaiah when he saw the Lord seated upon His throne? Hearing the call of the seraphs—"Holy, holy, holy is the LORD of hosts"—Isaiah cried out, "Woe is me! For I am lost; for I am a man of unclean lips" (Isaiah 6:3, 5). In the presence of God and His court, with the searing vision of God's holiness, shouldn't we also be frightened people of silent lips?

To answer these concerns, we have the First Petition. Here is God's direction that draws out our prayer. The First Petition is the choir's opening line, and it permits and expects us to pray harmoniously with others. Imagine that, by pure grace, you have passed the choir audition and you're in the choir room. Now the choir director gives you permission to sing. More than that, you're expected to sing. You can't be in the choir just to stand there in awe of the others.

The Lord's Prayer opens for us with permission to and expectation of singing our desires in the presence of God. We're commanded to sing with all the others whose voices reach Him. Luther explained this idea concerning prayer in the Large Catechism, saying that we pray according to the command of God, regardless of what our lives lack compared to the saints and their holy lives:

> For we let thoughts like these lead us astray and stop us: "I am not holy or worthy enough. If I were as godly and holy as St. Peter or St. Paul, then I would pray." But put such thoughts far away. For the same commandment

that applied to St. Paul applies also to me. The Second Commandment is given as much on my account as on his account. . . . You should say, "My prayer is as precious, holy, and pleasing to God as that of St. Paul or of the most holy saints . . . God does not consider prayer because of the person, but because of His Word and obedience to it." (Large Catechism, Part III, paragraphs 15, 16)

HEAVEN   HEAVEN

OUR FATHER —NAME

KINGDOM & POWER

KINGDOM COME

DELIVER US

WILL BE DONE

LEAD US NOT

DAILY BREAD

FORGIVENESS

EARTH

Therefore, we're commanded by the grace of God to pray, and by that, we're allowed a place in the heavenly choir that far exceeds our own expectations. What is astonishing to our self-centeredness is that the opening words of the prayer are not about our sinfulness, but rather about God's holiness. I would start with "I am a sinner." But He starts me with "Holy is Your name." God draws me out of my focus on my own failures and begins my prayer with His perfection. As our model of a journey suggests, prayer begins in heaven's glory as a remarkable invitation by God. We began prayer at the highest point with our Father in heaven, and our diagram of the prayer shows how the First Petition keeps us in the heavenly choir.

A Stream of Voices

Many people are fascinated by the rush of water over a rocky streambed. Perhaps you've tried to capture the wonder of the water flashing over the gravel by taking a picture of it. Some might look at the picture, see only rocks and water, a little sparkle perhaps, and ask, "You took this picture because . . .?" In a way, they're asking a valid question. A river is never caught in a single moment. To know a river, you have to sit beside it, wade through it, camp on its banks, and fall asleep beside it. There's a magic that draws us to streams, a magic that can't be held or captured in a single photograph.

So we come to the Lord's Prayer. Some might see it as a fixed picture of our conversation with God. It looks interesting perhaps, but hardly overwhelming. Like a picture of a stream you can hold in your hand, you might imagine that you've captured the whole experience after a few repetitions. All the words fit in a few phrases, and our memories can tuck it away.

But streams and prayers can't be caught. Both are living. Streams and prayers are a bit of both heaven and earth, coming together in one moment. Streams are last week's clouds and rain, and today they race over the stones. You watch a stream because you know this water may have traveled a hundred miles already and has hundreds more to go. You're fascinated with this one moment. You're caught between what is endless and what is only in this instant. Here is this one moment of the waterfall with these particular sparkling drops of water.

God draws me out of my focus on my own failures and begins my prayer with His perfection.

But this waterfall has been going on every minute of your entire life. You simply never saw it before. Yet, in this exact instant, at least for you, these drops have never sparkled in just this way.

So we pray in an endless stream of sparkling moments. The Lord's

Prayer draws us into a flow of praise that has been lifted up before the heavenly throne for centuries and beyond the counting of time. This stream has come from the voices of angels, the heavenly saints, and earthbound believers since long before we were born. For an instant, we're caught up with their voices when we remember these words, "hallowed be Thy name." This river of their praise is the constant stream of heaven. If we ever sleep in heaven, this praise of God will be the soothing whisper behind our dreams. Its laughter will wake us when our dreams are done.

While we capture a moment of this praise in the phrase "hallowed be Thy name," these words make us more than listeners. Streams call us. We take off our shoes and roll up our pant legs so we can wade in. We reach in for the brightest stone on the bottom. We sit on the rocks beside the stream just before it tumbles over the waterfall. We revel in the mist covering our face. Streams aren't content with people who only watch; they want to move us all in.

The praise of God that we overhear is a compelling stream—the voices of angels and saints are a perfect, sparkling symphony of glory to God. Yet, for all the completeness of heaven's praise, there is a winsome vacuum about it. Like a stream that is perfect by itself but somehow better if you are standing in it, so their praise welcomes us. We are the new stone over which their praise runs, laughing on its way to the throne of God. This is the rejoicing of the angels over each of us praying sinners who are found praying with them. The praise of angels and saints is the welcoming start of our prayer. The Spirit directs and enlivens our praying in this harmony. This Spirit-led symphony of voices compels us to become a part of their eternal river of praise.

Our Fellow Choir Members

In this river of praise, God directs us to pray by giving us the very words to sing. These words compel us to pray. As we begin, we're conscious of those we're joining. While we speak to God, we're also aware of all the others who are with us. Because we say, "Our Father who art in heaven," we recognize at least three ranks within the universal choir of prayer: the angels, the heavenly saints, and the saints on earth. We join in a triad of three perfectly balanced groups, a three-part chord.

The Heavenly Angels

We have joined first with the angels and all the heavenly beings in their song. Listen to some of heaven's music from the Book of Revelation:

> Then I looked, and I heard around the throne and the
> living creatures and the elders the voice of many angels,
> numbering myriads of myriads and thousands of thou-
> sands, saying with a loud voice, "Worthy is the Lamb who
> was slain, to receive power and wealth and wisdom and
> might and honor and glory and blessing!" And I heard
> every creature in heaven and on earth and under the earth
> and in the sea, and all that is in them, saying, "To Him who
> sits on the throne and to the Lamb be blessing and honor
> and glory and might forever and ever!" (5:11–13)

The chorus goes on and on. The four living creatures sing, "Holy, holy, holy, is the Lord God Almighty, who was and is and is to come" (Revelation 4:8). They and the twenty-four elders say, "Worthy are You, our Lord and God, to receive glory and honor and power, for You created all things, and by Your will they existed and were created" (Revelation 4:11). The angels around the throne fall on their faces and say, "Amen! Blessings and glory and wisdom and thanksgiving and honor and power and might be to our God forever and ever! Amen" (Revelation 7:12). All of these verses remind us of the pure, harmonious singing that surrounds our heavenly Father.

In our image of a three-note chord, let the angel voices be the highest note. Let's make the first note, the root, a C; then up a third to E, our second note; and end with a G. Angels make a perfect fifth step, the G at the top of the chord. Imagine their section hitting breathlessly the highest notes and holding them for an impossible length in perfect pitch.

Isn't it a wonder that, while listening to their perfect praise, God also listens intently to you, His beloved child? Isn't it stunning to think that as you begin the First Petition, the angel choirs, rather than drowning out your words, harmoniously accompany your feeble voice in prayer? Your whispered "hallowed be Thy name" is magnified by their chorus. They step aside and welcome you into their ranks. Martin

Chemnitz says of the first three petitions and our partnership with the angels:

> We are therefore taught to pray that this unity between
> the company of angels and of men may be begun in this
> life. We desire that we may progress toward and seek after
> that blessed communion. The angels readily and cheer-
> fully, without any stubbornness and resistance, but out of
> love and obedience, execute these things. . . . Therefore,
> we pray that this also may be begun in us.[8]

This makes prayer exceptional compared to the finest choir experience. It is no praise for a choir or its director when someone says, even with good intentions, "There are some wonderful voices in the choir, especially the third woman from the left. She really stands out." In a choir of wonderful voices, no single voice is supposed to be noticed. It's a choir, not a contest. It's only the whole that counts.

Think, then, of the choir to which our heavenly Father is listening in heaven. He's surrounded by harmonious sound, produced by angels and saints who do not compete with one another. Their voices are, to our ears at least, a solidly woven cloth of balanced sound. Into that perfect design, God incorporates our voice of prayer. Our "hallowed be Thy name" blends seamlessly into their ranks. We, though strangers to heaven by our nature, are welcomed home as though this heavenly praise and place were our native pitch.

Yet God hears us individually as we join in. He hears each separate voice and the nuance of that praise. Imagine the choir director pointing his baton at you and saying, "I heard that." That can't be good news. You must be flat or sharp, early or late. Something stands out. But God hears us in the kindest way. He points to each of us as we pray and says, "I heard that." Even in the midst of the angelic choir, He distinguishes our voices. He knows the background of the cry that colors our "hallowed be Thy name" in comparison to our neighbor's cry. He knows when you say these words courageously and with slim faith, out of pain, or fear, or repentance. He knows when you pray with the excited tones of rejoicing or thanks or certainty. Our Father recog-nizes the voice of each of His children as a good parent strains to hear

8   Martin Chemnitz, *Ministry, Word, and Sacraments: An Enchiridion*, trans. by Luther Poellot, J. A. O. Preus, and
    Georg Williams (St. Louis: Concordia, 2007), 46.

his or her child in a choir. While no parent could find just one voice in such a perfect choir, God does. In this choir of heaven, I never sing a nightmarish solo, and yet I'm never drowned beneath the perfection of others, even the perfect angels in heaven.

Pray even when
IT'S JUST TO SEE WHO'S THERE.

Elisha's servant saw only the enemy army surrounding his city one morning and he knew he was going to die. The Syrian army had surrounded them during the night and there was no escape. But Elisha simply assured his servant, "Do not be afraid, for those who are with us are more than those who are with them." Elisha prayed, "O Lord, please open his eyes that he may see." And the servant saw the horses and chariots of fire around Elisha (2 Kings 6:16–17).

As we join the choir in singing, it might be enough to ask for a glimpse, by faith, of the many who are already with us. Lord, let me see the ranks in the choir, the chariots of fire. Remind me of the many who are with me.

The Heavenly Saints

Along with the angelic choir, our Father is listening to the heaven-gathered saints. Revelation 7:15 describes them as those who are before the throne of God and serve Him day and night in His temple. Their chorus of praise is, "Salvation belongs to our God who sits on the throne and to the Lamb!" (Revelation 7:10). Revelation 22:3–4 shows the closeness of the saints with God as the new heaven is described: "The throne of God and of the Lamb will be in it, and His servants will worship Him. They will see His face, and His name will be on their foreheads." As we noted in the previous chapter, God the Father has seated all believers with Christ in the heavenly places (Ephesians 2:6). When we pray, we act on this promise and join our voices with those believers who are already truly there before God's throne.

Imagine who's praying with us. Your first words of the Lord's Prayer are joined by those who perhaps heard your very first words here on earth, parents or grandparents who have joined the heavenly chorus. They treasured your first words and repeated them for years. Now their prayers join yours in heaven, and your few small words of prayer are repeated by them in the presence of the heavenly Father. The enormous distance between us in space, time, and experience is now gone. In prayer, we are for those moments raising a common song, and we have a glimpse of us all joined in the same choir.

In prayer, we are for those moments raising a common song, and we have a glimpse of us all joined in the same choir.

This joining with the chorus of angels and saints is not restricted to our individual prayers; nor is it a novel idea. Prayer in company with the angels and saints is part of liturgical worship as shown in the words sung before we receive the Lord's Supper: "Therefore with angels and archangels and with all the company of heaven we laud and magnify Your glorious name, evermore praising You and saying . . ."[9] These words of praise lead us to sing: "Holy, holy, holy, Lord God of Sabaoth; heaven and earth are full of Thy glory, Hosanna, hosanna, hosanna in the highest. Blessed is He, blessed is He, blessed is He that cometh in the name of the Lord. Hosanna, hosanna, hosanna in the highest."[10] These words on the magnificence of God, with their focus on His holiness, are a perfect companion to the First Petition. With the holy company of saints and angels, we praise our most holy God.

In our analogy of a three-part chord, we can make the saints in heaven the middle tone. They're the E, a third up from the root of C, bridging the high and low notes. When we who are still on earth begin the chord with our lowest tone, they are the first harmony. The saints know perfectly our notes. They know how we have prayed the prayer in both sorrow and joy, faith and doubt, for they prayed with the same

9   *Lutheran Service Book: Altar Book* (St. Louis: Concordia, 2006), p. 264.

10 *Lutheran Service Book: Altar Book*, p. 245.

notes while on earth. But now they harmonize with us in higher tones. Safely with the Father in heaven, anticipating the resurrection of their bodies, they sing with new, higher notes of faith and waiting.

The Saints of Earth

The choir is nearly full with the angels and saints joining our own individual, timid voices. However, there is one more body of voices to hear. While we might imagine fairly easily the angels and saints joining us, we could forget the uncounted thousands, hundreds of thousands, and even millions of believers praying with us at the same moment. These are the voices scattered around the globe who are parallel to us. Their lives march in step with ours and even now they say the prayer exactly as we do. What an idea: in another corner of the world, in a language we'll never know, believers are speaking this petition at the same moment as we are. Imagine just for a moment the breadth of all nations from which God hears their prayers, along with ours, saying, "Hallowed be Thy name." We as Christians are never alone, especially in our prayer lives. Though we may pray in a closet, we hear the echoes of the family of believers just beyond our door, across the globe.

Though we may pray in a closet, we hear the echoes of the family of believers just beyond our door, across the globe.

Our theme for the prayer is that of a journey, stretching from heaven to earth and returning to heaven again. Our use of the heavenly chorus especially shows this heaven-to-earth journey. But here we can pause on the journey to appreciate the breadth of the believers who join us. The thousands and even millions who speak the prayer are a restless, constant wave, pushing against the boundary shore between heaven and earth. Their words are not a futile or mindless repetition, ignorant waves crashing against an unmoving rock. They speak the words to which our Father has already opened His ears and heart. Like the constant waves on a shore, the saints make a perfect chorus, familiar but changing in tone with each echo.

Keeping with our theme of the chorus of prayer, perhaps we may see this First Petition as a canon, a song sung in a round. These few words, "hallowed be Thy name," are taken up in turn by the angels, the saints in heaven, the saints on earth, and you. The never-ending, ever-changing choir sings a constant theme, which we have just enlarged by our part. Each part—angels, saints in heaven, saints still on earth—welcomes us into the choir.

Our challenge is to hear these unseen angels and saints as we pray. We already have this vision of the invisible in other ways. The mother and father awaiting their unborn child paint bright colors in the second bedroom, buy a crib, and celebrate with a baby shower long before the child is born. They put money in savings for college and even begin to pray for their future daughter- or son-in-law. They shape much of their lives in view of a child they've not yet seen.

It is bountiful grace that opens the door for your voice to be included.

When we see the breadth and range of voices that join us in our prayer, we're caught up in the glory of that moment. We can shape this moment of prayer in light of those we haven't yet seen. Prayer is an instant we wish would never end. For one long moment, stop worrying, stop carrying the burden alone, stop filling your mind with the worries and temptations of this world. Stop acting as less than the child of God you are. Now, for one lasting moment, join the hosts of heaven, the saints ahead of us, and the saints around us in praise. For one lingering moment, step into the sparkling river of heaven's praise. When we pray this petition especially, we pause in the shining light of God. In His light, we are warmed, but not scorched; we're brightly lit, but not blinded; we're called to God, but not accused. Let this be a long, shining moment of praise.

Our joining in the Lord's Prayer brings us into invisible, yet real contact with those saints and angels who are saying the prayer at this moment. Think, then, of the chorus into which God places your prayer. It is bountiful grace that opens the door for your voice to be included. It is further grace that assures each of us that our God gladly hears each voice in the chorus.

What Shall I Sing?

Now that we've been ushered into our place within this mighty choir, the glory of the setting might tempt us to listen without uttering a word ourselves. This would be especially true if we could catch the smallest glimpse of God the Father on His throne, or of Jesus as He is pictured in Revelation 1:12–16. There Jesus blazes with eyes as fire, hair white as snow, and a voice like the sound of many waters. John does what we would do, saying, "When I saw Him, I fell at His feet as though dead" (1:17a). But the words and actions of Jesus revive John and us: "But He laid His right hand on me, saying, 'Fear not'" (1:17b).

This is the reassuring vision of Jesus we need as we begin to hallow His name. The glorious holiness of God separates us from Him, but still He calls us to pray. The God from whom I shrink in fear puts His hand on me and says, "Fear not." Given this tension, we begin the prayer with God's direction, "hallowed be Thy name." This petition suggests that there is an element of God's holiness which is not yet fully realized. Yet, our glimpse of our Father in His heavenly glory shows nothing is lacking in Him or His heaven. God's holiness is certainly complete in itself, as Luther explains the petition in his catechism.[11] Along with the element of wishing in this First Petition, there is also an exalting, declarative aspect: "Holy is Your name here in heaven. Perfect is its worship and power. May it be so also on earth as it is in heaven."

What, then, do we wish to be completed on earth for the honor of God's name? The Greek verb ἁγιάζω, *hagiazo*, "hallow," is used in twenty-five verses in the New Testament, though only seven of those verses are in the Gospels. Some Bible versions translate the verb as to make holy, dedicate, sanctify, and to treat as holy.[12] Generally, God purifies or makes holy. For example, 1 Thessalonians 5:23 says, "Now may the God of peace Himself sanctify you completely." God shows His holiness to the world by the expected glory of His name. This is seen in Jesus' own prayer to the Father concerning the disciples in John 17:17: "Sanctify them in the truth; Your word is truth." This work of God is done through the Son and the Spirit as seen in 1 Corinthians 1:2, "to those sanctified in Christ Jesus," and 1 Corinthians 6:11, "But you were washed, you were sanctified, you were justified in the name of the Lord Jesus Christ and by the Spirit of our God."

This sanctification is God's own work, glorifying His own name.

---

11 Luther writes in the Large Catechism, "Yes, it [God's name] is always holy in its nature, but in our use it is not holy. . . . For He will not hear anything more dear to Him than that His honor and praise is exalted above everything else and that His Word is taught in its purity and is considered precious and dear" (Part III, paragraphs 37, 48).

12 These seven verses are Matthew 6:9; 23:17, 19; Luke 11:2; John 10:36; 17:17, 19.

But it's a costly glory, bought through the cross. The Book of Hebrews uses this verb, *hagiazo,* "hallow," more than any New Testament book—seven times in six verses.[13] The focus is on the sacrifice of Christ's blood, such as in Hebrews 10:10: "By that will we have been sanctified through the offering of the body of Jesus Christ once for all." This sacrifice of the Son binds us to the Father, as Hebrews 2:11 explains: "For He who sanctifies and those who are sanctified all have once source. That is why He is not ashamed to call them brothers." Just as we call upon God as Father only through His Son's work, so we approach His holiness and ask for its sanctifying work only through the Son.

While it's true that God and His name are always holy of themselves, let's not imagine that this work of sanctifying was a painless, natural part of God. It's too easy to think that all we're saying in the First Petition is, "Father, Your name is holy of itself. Now make us live holy lives as we should." This understanding omits the work of sanctification already done in Christ, which is the clear focus of the majority of the New Testament verses dealing with this verb "sanctify." When we praise His holiness and work of sanctification, we are reminded of His suffering as the rejected lamb. Hebrews 13:11–15 reminds us of these themes of the praise of the holiness of God and His name brought by those who are seeking God in His holy city:

> For the bodies of those animals whose blood is brought
> into the holy places by the high priest as a sacrifice for
> sin are burned outside the camp. So Jesus also suffered
> outside the gate in order to sanctify the people through
> His own blood. Therefore let us go to Him outside the
> camp and bear the reproach He endured. For here we
> have no lasting city, but we seek the city that is to come.
> Through Him then let us continually offer up a sacrifice
> of praise to God, that is, the fruit of lips that acknowledge
> His name.

We stand with the saints and angels in awe of His willingness to sanctify us this way. Hebrews 9:13 reminds us that the blood of goats and bulls and the ashes of a heifer were formerly that which cleansed. Now the Son has taken the place of blood and ashes. Isn't it astonishing

---

13 These seven times are Hebrews 2:11, where it is translated as "sanctify" and used twice; 9:13; 10:10, 14, 29; and 13:12.

that He whom we praise in glorious heaven creates the holy city—this heavenly place of praise—because He has been as the sacrificed body burned outside the camp? We sing a chorus of honor to Him in the enduring city because He was willing to be cast out of His own city. Our saying of the petition grows this way: "Father, Your name is holy of itself. We praise You through the gracious work of Your holy Son, who cleansed us. Holy is Your name and holy is the work of Your Son. Cause us to live holy lives as we follow Him."

GROW THE TREE OF A GOOD NAME

"A good name is to be chosen rather than great riches" (Proverbs 22:1). Our names are small echoes of the perfect name of God, which we praise. While we praise the Father's name, we can also ask that He would straighten and protect our names.

Newly planted trees are braced up straight and have a protecting fence around them. The reputations of our names are like small trees, in need of God's guarding fence around them and His bracing to make them grow straight. Lord, let my name grow straight and strong, safe in the shadow of Your own great name.

What Shall I Call Him?

This holiness of God that we praise is connected to the name of God, "Our Father." We say, in essence, "May Your name be praised, glorified, and effective in every realm of heaven and earth." But how are we to honor and glorify His name?

I think that our earlier image of a heavenly choir helps in this regard. The choir of saints and angels sings constantly before the throne of God with a sparkling range of voices. There must be a collective sound and yet a distinctive variety. All sing the same melody or its supporting harmony. Yet, it's fair to imagine that we could tell the angels' voices from the saints. (All of this is, of course, necessarily squinting through a mirror dimly [1 Corinthians 13:12] since we are on this side of heaven. But it seems reasonable to imagine that there are different sounds within a central melody and distinctions possible between the various singers of heaven.) Within this choir, our simple strain of "Our Father who art in heaven, hallowed be Thy name" is welcomed by the choir and noticed by our Father. The confusion of languages from Babel (Genesis 11) is now over. All the voices of heaven and earth sing one song.

The name of God is commonly understood as a synonym for the completeness of God, all that He is. When we ask that the name of God be hallowed and revered, we're inviting the chorus of voices with whom we are praising God to remind us of the many names by which He has revealed Himself. Each voice might take up one of the names as a particular note and sing it in a distinctive way. We might hear in a dominant melody line perhaps these opening tones, "I AM" and "I AM WHO I AM" (Exodus 3:14). Ringing clearly next to this lead are "Lord," "Jesus," and "Christ," the names of praise lifted to the Father concerning His Son in Philippians 2:10–11: "That at the name of Jesus every knee should bow, in heaven and on earth and under the earth,

Think of these seven titles of "I am" as a musical round; the first begins quietly by itself, with each of the others being added until the full number is heard.

and every tongue confess that Jesus is Lord, to the glory of God the Father." The names "Father" and "Spirit" complete our first impression of the name of God. These seven are like the essential notes of a melody line. They are the core of our remembrance of the nature of God.

Yet, a complete symphony is glorious because of the variety of instruments and the wonderfully unique sounds each makes. You might not want an entire CD of tuba tunes or cymbal clashes, but we appreciate their contributions to the overall sound. In your prayers for the hallowing and glorifying of God's name, listen for the occasional voice, the singular name of one person of the Trinity, or His distinctive work. We can't capture all the biblical names here, but notice the following names, which are grouped like an intentional, harmonious chord, the highest and lowest notes of this spreading song. Isaiah gives us the Christmas tone of Isaiah 9:6, "Wonderful Counselor, Mighty God, Everlasting Father, Prince of Peace." There are the names of God from the hymns in Luke 1, "Savior" (v. 47), "He who is Mighty" (v. 49), "Lord God of Israel" (v. 68), and "the Most High" (v. 76). In John's Gospel, we have Jesus' ringing statements of being "I am." He is "the bread of life" (6:35), "the light of the world" (8:12), "the door of the sheep" (10:7), "the good shepherd" (10:11), "the resurrection and the life" (11:25), "the way, the truth, and the life" (14:6), and "the true vine" (15:1). Think of these seven titles of "I am" as a musical round; the first begins quietly by itself, with each of the others being added until the full number is heard. Hear the overflowing chorus, the rushing of voices like water over seven stones. The first names and their notes quietly fall away until just the one is left. Then they begin again.

While we've drawn on many texts for these names, Revelation especially gives rich chords surrounding the name of God. Revelation 5:5–6 supplies these contrasting names, "the Lion of the tribe of Judah," "the Root of David," and the "Lamb." Capturing a tone of majesty, Revelation 19 lists the three names of the rider of the white horse: He "is called Faithful and True" (v. 11); "the name by which He is called is The Word of God" (v. 13); "On His robe and on His thigh He has a name written, King of kings and Lord of lords" (v. 16). Faithful and True, Word of God, King of kings, and Lord of lords. You can imagine the grandeur of this chorus in the mouths of the angels and saints. Revelation closes in 22:16 with these descriptions of Jesus: "I am the root and the descendant of David, the bright morning star." In response to these and His promise to return soon, the Church sings, "Amen. Come, Lord Jesus!" (Revelation 22:20).

There are certainly many other names that are significant in identifying the nature and work of God. But the ones presented here are intriguing for their nearness to one another in Scripture, making a cohesive chord, distinct yet complementary. Listen to their echo as you pray, "Hallowed be Thy name." Linger over His name, and hear these notes magnify one another.

The Living Song

"Hallowed be Thy name" is the song that stays with us. More than any melody, this petition repeats itself. The singers above us, before us, and beyond us hallow His name endlessly. Their music draws us into the heavenly choir. With this petition, we're asking God that the song from heaven's court would become our song also in daily life and that we might be part of the choir. We pray to know His words and to live them. We want to be found singing His praise at any random moment. "Hallowed be Thy name" is the song we sing when we think no one is listening. It's our song when we know we're being watched and heard. We pray that the Lord would give us holy lives in tune with His own glory and that we would become living and holy sacrifices to God (Romans 12:1).

Luther reminds us to hallow God's name by the Word rightly taught and our lives rightly lived.[14] In this petition, we're asking God to help us follow the music that He has written. We pray, "Have me sing only when I should. Keep me silent when my solo is over. Let me both speak Your praise and be silent to know that You are God."

Join the chorus that soars above us. Be drawn into this eternal stream. Be astonished that those whose praise of God is perfect welcome your voice. Be even more amazed that the One who is perfect hears your feeble voice among theirs. Let our song of thanks and wonder be for the Son whose blood made us holy before the Father. Let His work be never-ending in tuning our lives to His song. The choir of heaven and earth opens to receive us. Together with all the choir of heaven and earth, we sing, "Hallowed be Thy name."

---

14 "God's name is indeed holy in itself. But we pray in this petition that it may become holy among us also. How is this done? When the Word of God is taught in its truth and purity and we as the children of God also lead holy lives in accordance with it" (Small Catechism, Lord's Prayer, First Petition).

CHAPTER THREE

{ "You Come Too" }

IN THE POEM "THE PASTURE," ROBERT FROST INVITES US TO JOIN
HIM IN DOING CHORES ON HIS VERMONT FARM. There's work to do,
but he doesn't want to do it alone. Hear his invitation. Feel the warmth
of his outstretched hand, especially in the last, repeated line of each
verse.

> I'm going out to clear the pasture spring;
> I'll only stop to rake the leaves away
> (And wait to watch the water clear, I may):
> I sha'n't be gone long. You come too.
>
> I'm going out to fetch the little calf
> That's standing by the mother.
> It's so young,
> It totters when she licks it with her tongue.
> I sha'n't be gone long. You come too.[15]

Don't you want to come along? Clearing the spring is more than
a chore. When the water flows again, who knows what we'll see. Come
on, let's see it together. The little calf stumbles, and we'll laugh at its
knobby, shaking legs taking those first steps. But laughter is always
better when it's shared. We won't be gone long. Won't you come too?

15   Robert Frost, *North of Boston* (New York: Henry Holt and Company, 1914), frontispiece.

In the poem, Frost is a farmer speaking perhaps to his grandchildren. He has chores to do, and the grandchildren are lucky to go with him. But you might read these words another way. Perhaps this is a child who is tugging at his father. Anyone can clear a pasture spring and chase a calf. Even a child can do it, but he doesn't want to do it alone. The child's promise is sincere: "I shan't be gone long." His hand is already pulling on his father's sleeve. He says, "I have to go do my chores. It won't be long. Come with me. It'll be better if you come too."

The Second and Third Petitions of our Lord's Prayer are a turning point. After we've reveled in the Father's invitation to speak to Him even while He is in heaven ("Our Father who art in heaven") and been welcomed into the choir of praise that surrounds Him ("hallowed be Thy name"), we turn toward earth ("Thy kingdom come, Thy will be done on earth as it is in heaven"). In part, we're somewhat reluctant to remember earth, its needs, and its failures because heaven is perfect and glorious—we could stay forever on "hallowed be Thy name." But now the petitions of the prayer and our thoughts both turn to earth. As Frost's poem suggests, we have work that has to be done. We don't want to be gone long. After all, heaven is our Father's home and ours too. But we take the Father's hand and ask that He would do on earth as He does in heaven. We want to take a bit of the glory and order that we have glimpsed in heaven and see it brought here on earth. We can't do this ourselves. So we ask our Father to come. We shan't be gone long, Father—You come too.

We take the Father's hand and ask that He would do on earth as He does in heaven.

The Journey's Next Long Step

This pairing of the Second and Third Petitions gives our journey within the Lord's Prayer its first long stride toward earth. At the beginning with "Our Father," we leap up to heaven as the Father hears our words. But with these petitions of kingdom and will, we take the long downward step on our diagram. In the First Petition, we lingered at our Father's home while we were drawn into the stream of heaven's song. Now it's time to bind heaven and earth together.

As noted in the previous chapter, the praise and hallowing of God's name happens both in heaven and on earth. The concluding

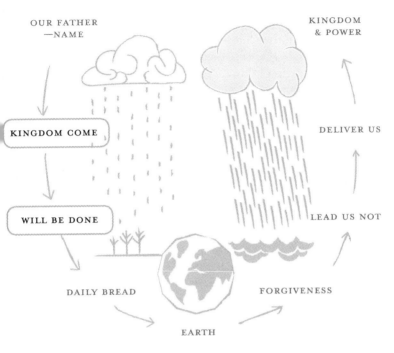

HEAVEN   HEAVEN

OUR FATHER
—NAME

KINGDOM
& POWER

KINGDOM COME

DELIVER US

WILL BE DONE

LEAD US NOT

DAILY BREAD

FORGIVENESS

EARTH

words of the Third Petition, "on earth as it is in heaven," are concerned with all three of the petitions thus far. Each of the petitions binds together heaven and earth, and our viewpoint widens to take in the whole expanse. In heaven and on earth we're looking for the same work of God to be done. However, our journey turns more decisively toward earth with the Second and Third Petitions because there is a greater sense of movement with the phrase "Thy kingdom come" and the reminder "on earth as it is in heaven." With the Introduction and First Petition, we begin in the clear realms of our Father in heaven. Soon, with the Fourth Petition, we will find ourselves firmly on earth, standing beneath the daily showers of heavenly gifts. The Second and Third Petitions of kingdom and will are the transition of the journey. They hold together heaven and earth. We've just seen a bit of God's kingdom in heaven. Now we're anxious that more of His glory would come over us here on earth. These petitions are the child's firm hold on the heavenly Father, urging, "You come too."

In this chapter, we bring the Second and Third Petitions into a single step on our diagram. This is the perspective of Luke's version of the Lord's Prayer (11:2): "Father, hallowed be Your name. Your kingdom come." The Third Petition, "Thy will be done," is not present in the earliest manuscripts of Luke.[16] Yet, the prayer in Luke is a complete journey and prayer despite not listing this petition. The ideas contained in the Third Petition are assumed under the Second so that the coming kingdom includes also the will of the Father being done.

A Longing View

In chapter 1, I drew the picture of a mountaintop overlook where we focus outside of ourselves. We stand on a ten-thousand-foot mountain pass, brushing against the clouds and looking over the peaks nearby. There are no mirrors at this overlook, but there is a great deal of looking and longing. Imagine having a house on this mountain. You would wake up every morning to an incredible view. I doubt you would ever want to leave, certainly not on Monday morning just to go to work. That is our First Petition—the praise of the Father's name, our voice echoing within the heavenly choir, singing, "Hallowed be Thy name." Who would ever want to leave?

This is all a wonderful image, but the reality of your house is probably less glorious than this view of heaven. Your picture window looks out on a flat square of mostly brown lawn, with more dandelions than grass, bounded by a patched asphalt street. You see only the dark bottom of the clouds, and your neighbor's sagging fence is your horizon. What happened to the mountain view and your home where eagles soar? We were just in the heavenly choir and we imagined seeing what they see. Why can't we stay with them? In the Second and Third Petitions, we're drawn downward by the chores that call us home.

This transition from the heavenly choir to our earthly chores is like a tour of homes. In the fall, you buy your tickets to the Parade

16 The challenging, brief text which omits "Your will be done on earth as it is on heaven" is supported by the important manuscripts Vaticanus of the fourth century and Papyrus 75 of the third century. Most other manuscripts, especially the later ones, include the words of the Third Petition. It is possible and very likely that the two versions of the Lord's Prayer in Matthew 6 and Luke 11 reflect two different contexts in which Jesus said the prayer. He speaks first in Matthew to a large audience and later in Luke to His disciples. The key is that the prayer is a complete journey in Luke even without the Third Petition. The will of God is assumed under the kingdom.

of Homes and walk through eight perfect houses. The smell of new carpet lingers on you like perfume. You've never seen so many flower arrangements on dining room tables or fountains bubbling in backyard parks. But you know you have to go home. Your brown carpet with its worn path meets you at the front door. Your dining room table has no bouquet of fresh flowers but rather a few dirty dishes from supper, three bills with their envelopes torn open, and someone's coat draped over one of the chairs. Stepping into your backyard gives you only the sound of your deck creaking from that pair of loose boards. Do this often enough, and you'll stop going on any more house tours.

But imagine if you met someone at the door of the last mansion you visit. He's not the owner; he is the man who built the house himself and he asks how you like it. You assure him it's fantastic, the best house you've ever seen. He asks what your house is like. "Nothing like this," you tell him. "Oh," he says, "would you like to make some changes?" "Well, it could never be like yours," you reply. "No," he says, "but we could get a start on it." You ask, "Would you really want to work on my house?" "Of course," he says. "Well then," you say, "let's go home. And you come too."

> There is One who built heaven and earth, the Carpenter who meets us at the door. He knows our house and where the remodeling should begin.

We may feel the same way after beginning the Lord's Prayer, with its wonderful opening of the welcoming Father and the glorious praise of His name by heaven and ourselves. That glimpse of heaven is like visiting the perfect mansion; we envy the saints and angels for their flawless home because our own world offers a worn, brown welcome at best. Torn bills and creaking joints try to drown out the praise we heard in heaven. But there is One who built heaven and earth, the Carpenter who meets us at the door. He knows our house and where the remodeling should begin. Given His perfect work in heaven and His willingness to come to earth, how can we not ask Him, "Will You come too?"

"Thy kingdom come, Thy will be done on earth as it is in heaven" is the transition from glory to our earthly home. It lets us move slowly from heaven back to earth, where daily bread and forgiveness come. These petitions let us enjoy heaven's chorus of praise and their welcome of our part in singing. As we walk with the Carpenter toward the remodeling that needs to be done, we should probably hum these two petitions to the echo of "hallowed be Thy name," the tune of praise that we just heard. We're now asking that our Father would come with us to tune our world according to His own pitch so that our melody would continue on earth as it did in heaven. We realize that our world cannot become a perfect showcase of His holiness, kingdom, and will. However, the heavenly choir's song is still with us, and our heavenly home still draws us. "Father, bring us nearer to Yourself, Your name, Your praise, and Your home even while we're here on earth." These petitions invite us to explore our Father's kingdom, which is already around us. In these words, we go from lingering praise to solid work in a kingdom that's not yet finished. Finally, we're assured that when His kingdom comes, we'll come too. These petitions remind us that this world is just for these few days; a lasting home is coming.

GROW WITH THE ENERGY OF EVEN THE ANT

"Go to the ant, O sluggard; consider her ways, and be wise" (Proverbs 6:6). There's work to be done! While we ask God to bring His kingdom and will, there's something for us to do also. Solomon points us to the ant—so small, yet so wise and so busy. Even the ant knows that winter is coming and there's work to be done. If you are at least as wise as the ant, then wake up! Today, you might be exhausted and imagine there's so little you can do. Go to the ant! Lord, let me be at least as wise as the ant and let me do at least the little that even the ant gets done today.

There's A Whole World Waiting—You Come Too

This morning, as I walked our dog, Abby, we met two baby birds walking in the middle of the street. They were killdeers, the birds you often see walking, dragging one wing as though they were hurt, and then flying away when you get too close. However, these were babies, so small they could have fit together in the palm of my hand. They were simply wandering in the middle of the street. Abby and I were only a few feet away, while the babies' parents were about twenty feet or so from us, calling to them. These tiny birds made little cheeping sounds and were as willing to come toward Abby, our curious beagle, as they were to head toward their parents. Even when a car came down the street, they still wandered in the middle of the road.

These baby birds acted as though Sixth Street in Cedar Grove, Wisconsin, was the Garden of Eden. They had no idea that beagles or Buicks even existed, let alone that such things could ever hurt them. They were simply living in the joy of meandering through an absolutely wonderful June morning, no clouds, seventy-three degrees, and a few puddles from yesterday's rain. Perhaps if they could have spoken to their parents they would have said, "What a perfect world." To each other, they might have said, "Let's go see it!" and to their parents, "You come too." (When I left them that day, they were still marching happily up Sixth Street on a perfect morning.)

I hope that when we pray the Lord's Prayer, we do so in joy and with a bit of excitement, just like those baby killdeers parading down Sixth Street. We're children still opening the wonders of the garden. True, we're on the far side of Eden, but there are still new mornings to be discovered. Our Father still invites His children to find what He's planted. While the old, evil foe is around us, there is also a place for exploring. If our Father protects two happily wandering killdeer, won't He much more take care of you? If God puts curious beagles on leashes, so they can only sniff but not bite, won't He also keep on a leash the worst beasts we might face? While our old enemy is a "roaring lion, seeking someone to devour" (1 Peter 5:8), remember that absolute power belongs entirely to our Father, who will "restore, confirm, strengthen, and establish you. To Him be the dominion forever and ever. Amen" (1 Peter 5:10–11).

The baby killdeers are a fair analogy for us in the Lord's Prayer. Birds are creatures of heaven, but when they're babies, they can only walk on earth. I don't think the little birds that morning could have flown an inch. But they were happy enough to walk. Flying would come later. When we pray, we're reminded that we're really creatures of heaven ourselves. By pure grace, one day we will all be changed, the perishable putting on the imperishable and the mortal putting on the immortal (1 Corinthians 15:51–53), and we will be lifted into the clouds to be with Christ and the resurrected saints (1 Thessalonians 4:17). But now we walk on earth. We know by faith that one day we'll fly, but today we're still just walking.

When we pray, "Thy kingdom come, Thy will be done on earth as it is in heaven," we're asking in part that we might see the reflections of heaven that are still here on earth. We pray that we would gladly accept heavenly June days, sunshine, clear skies, and seventy-three degrees. We pray that God would keep us from focusing on the clouds still over the horizon and that we would not imagine dangers that don't exist or fear the enemies He has already put on a leash. Our prayer remembers that Jesus' ministry already announced the arrival of the kingdom of God (Mark 1:14–15). It is the kingdom of God and His gracious will that give His children their perfect days.

We greet that morning, take our Father's hand, and say, "I want to know this world of Yours. Lead me into all You have made."

Part of our prayer is asking that we recognize perfect June mornings as a promise of His coming kingdom and will. Ephesians 1:18–19 speaks of this when Paul prays that, "having the eyes of your hearts enlightened, . . . you may know what is the hope to which He has called you, what are the riches of His glorious inheritance in the saints, and what is the immeasurable greatness of His power toward us who believe."

Jesus repeatedly tells the disciples that the kingdom of heaven belongs to those who become like little children (Matthew 18:3–4; 19:14; Mark 9:33–37; Luke 9:46–48). We pray that our Father would lead us into each day He has planned for us. Here we're the children of faith. Our Father protects the birds and the lilies, so we trust He will protect us also (Matthew 6:25–34). Our Father says, "Here is My kingdom and My will every new morning. Come into it with Me." We greet that morning, take our Father's hand, and say, "I want to know this world of Yours. Lead me into all You have made."

You Come Too—If I *Have* To Go

I've been speaking of cloudless mornings in June. But maybe it's the fifth gray January day in a row for you right now. No one would mistake your world for the Garden of Eden. Good news. There is another side to "Thy kingdom come," one that fits us when we're far from the garden.

"I want you to come with me, though I would much rather that neither of us had to go at all."

When have you thought that way?

Was it when you were about to go to school for the first time? You asked your mother or father to come too, if they were sure that you had to go. Perhaps it was leaving high school and going to college or into the military. You wanted your best friend to come to the same school or to join up with you. It was when you had to go into the doctor's office for surgery. You hoped that your spouse, your sister, or one of your children would volunteer to go with you, right up to the operating door if possible.

These are the times when we drag our feet, look for any excuse, and argue that we don't really need to go. Only when we're cornered do we settle for this compromise, "If I have to go, you come too." So with a tight grip, we walk to the bus, the door, or the hospital. If I have to go, you're coming with me.

One dimension of our prayer, "Thy kingdom come, Thy will be done on earth as it is in heaven," has this emotion. We would much rather stay where we have just been, enjoying the chorus of heaven. We would rather linger in the company of angels and archangels, but the prayer begins to move us reluctantly to earth where we know conflict is waiting. The psalmists cry out for us when they ache for one more day in the court of God. Psalm 26:8: "O LORD, I love the habitation of Your house and the place where Your glory dwells." Our prayer would be simply that of Psalm 27:4: "One thing have I asked of the LORD, that will I seek after: that I may dwell in the house of the LORD all the days of my life, to gaze upon the beauty of the LORD and to inquire in His temple." What could compare to even the fragment of heaven we have imagined? We agree with Psalm 84:1: "How lovely is Your dwelling place, O LORD of hosts!"

But the course of this river of prayer runs downhill. Remember last chapter's analogy about the laughing, singing stream that draws you toward it? We're pulled into the river of praise to God and covered by Him in the First Petition of the prayer. But like every stream, this one leads from heaven to earth. The laughing mountain stream, sparkling and gurgling without a care, finally has to settle down, grow wide and slow, turn a bit darker, pool behind a dam, energize a power plant. It's all part of being a river.

As children of God, we find ourselves led to work by the Second and Third Petitions. Certainly there is work in the hallowing of God's name. But these two petitions lead us to the battle surrounding the name, kingdom, and will of God. Martin Luther makes this clear in his Large Catechism, stating that God's hallowed name and coming kingdom have "summed up all that deals with God's honor and our salvation" (Part III, paragraph 60). The prayer for the will of God then faces toward the attacks that come against these two treasures. The evil trinity of devil, world, and flesh battle us, the devil commanding the others, so that "he chafes and rages as a fierce enemy with all his power and might. He marshals all his subjects and, in addition, enlists the world and our own flesh as his allies" (Part III, paragraph 62).

Luther's hymn "A Mighty Fortress Is Our God" sums up our feeling toward this battle and our chances in it: "The old evil foe Now means deadly woe; Deep guile and great might Are his dread arms in fight; On earth is not his equal" (*LSB* 656:1). What chance do we have against this enemy? We can only run to our Father as the battle approaches, take His strong hand, and say, "You come too." Then we can sing with Luther, "With might of ours can naught be done, Soon were our loss effected; But for us fights the valiant One, Whom God Himself elected. Ask ye, Who is this? Jesus Christ it is, Of Sabaoth Lord, And there's none other God; He holds the field forever" (stanza 2).

Though this war against Satan rages worldwide, our first focus is on the battle within ourselves. It is in our own fear and impending despair that God's will and kingdom have to reign. Repeatedly God reminds His children that He is with them with a power that overwhelms their enemies, "Fear not, for I am with you; be not dismayed, for I am your God; I will strengthen you, I will help you, I will uphold you with My righteous right hand" (Isaiah 41:10). Jesus reassures the Father's children in Luke 12:32, "Fear not, little flock, for it is your Father's good pleasure to give you the kingdom." The child's trembling, reluctant steps are upheld by a Father's strong hand and His assurance, "I am with you. I have walked through this danger already. It's all right. You come too."

The very name of Jesus, which has been our previous petition's concern, is a comfort here. We asked that the One named Immanuel will be praised and now ask that He will come with His kingdom. But His name Immanuel is our assurance that His kingdom will come. "Behold, the virgin shall conceive and bear a son, and they shall call His name Immanuel (which means, God with us)" (Matthew 1:23). We're asking the One who is "with us" to be with us in His kingdom and will. Perhaps we should insert Immanuel between the First and Second Petitions as a reminder of the confidence of our request. "Hallowed be Thy name. O Immanuel, certainly Thy kingdom and Thy will shall be done, on earth where You have already come and will come again."

When we ask God to come with His kingdom, He's more than ready. He's already far ahead of us. We're not asking a sleeping grandfather to leave his comfortable chair and come on some childish adventure that he'll humor for just a few minutes. We're not calling a father who has three phone calls to return, a computer screen waiting, a paper to be read, and dinner before him. That father may come, but only for a minute. Our prayer goes to the One who never leaves us and who closes Matthew's Gospel with the unending words, "And behold, I am with you always, to the end of the age" (28:20). When we as children call Him to come, He assures us, "I have already come, and I am already there ahead of you. I am coming again. Of course My kingdom and will shall come."

Remember Me When You Come into Your Kingdom

Most children welcome their father's homecoming. I hope you've lived in a house where "Dad's home!" is the start of something good. "Dad's home!" means now we can eat, now we can celebrate. But perhaps for you, there were some days when you dreaded the words "Dad's home." Something went wrong that day. The dent you put in the car, the broken window, or the angry neighbor was waiting for Dad when he came home. While you had your explanations ready, you knew none of them would ever work. Your older brother warned, "Dad will be home any minute. You think you're in trouble now? Just wait till then."

When Dad did roll up the driveway, where did you go? Did you race up to his car and ask him how his day was? Hardly. Maybe your escape was to run up to your room, or that place in the woods, or off to study, trying to look responsible. It would be natural for us to feel much of this same dread when we pray for the kingdom and will of

God to come. Some of the Gospel images of the approaching kingdom of God include those who are cast out into utter darkness with weeping and gnashing of teeth (Matthew 8:12; 25:30). Jesus' condemnation is summed up in, "Depart from Me, all you workers of evil!" (Luke 13:27). We dread standing in the horrible company of those lost souls and fallen angels, hearing, "Depart from Me, you cursed, into the eternal fire prepared for the devil and his angels" (Matthew 25:41). Before we too easily say, "Thy kingdom come," let's remember that as He came once with the flood, so He will come again with fire, the heavens and earth "being kept until the day of judgment and destruction of the ungodly" (2 Peter 3:7).

He invites them to the front row when He comes and encourages them to cry out, "Remember me when You come into Your Kingdom!"

This is the judgment that comes over all men. In the face of such judgment, we would, I imagine, shrink back into the crowd. Let others be judged first. Let God take as little notice of us as possible. Left to ourselves, on that final day we'll be looking for the very last row farthest from the throne. Who wants to stand out on the Day of Judgment?

That's what makes "Thy kingdom come, Thy will be done on earth as it is in heaven" such a bold request. Think of the repentant thief on the cross (Luke 23:40–43). Wouldn't he be the last person wanting to be noticed by a righteous king in His kingdom? Wouldn't you expect that he would shrink back into the shadows, dreading what's to come?

Yet this man, guilty as anyone, wants to be noticed when Jesus' kingdom comes. He admits that his wretched life deserves a miserable death. But he is a man who understands the nature of the King and His kingdom. This Jesus is crowned, even by the thorns. This King will live, despite the spears. This King will remember him, a complete criminal He met on the day of His death. It would be so easy for us to imagine Jesus blackening His memory of everyone from that day, including those who rightly died with Him. He could avoid any association with them in His glory, like a famous person denying any association with childhood friends, especially those who have turned into criminals.

Does anyone really expect an American president on his inauguration day to place on the reviewing stand his old neighbor who lived beside him in a little apartment for just a week and later was sentenced to life imprisonment for murder? What a hopeless request.

But this King remembers thieves and welcomes murderers. When the thief on the cross asked, "Remember me when You come into Your kingdom," Jesus promised more than a distant memory. "Today you will be with Me in Paradise," He said (Luke 23:42–43). The thief understood the grace of the King. He has a place of grace for criminals in His kingdom. He invites them to the front row when He comes and encourages them to cry out, "Remember me when You come into Your Kingdom!" With Him, there is no hopeless question mark to those words, no futile, "Remember me?" Our cry is a confident, "You will remember me. May Your kingdom come and Your gracious will be done." You'll come again, and You promised You would be coming soon (Revelation 22:20). Because of Your grace alone, we dare say, "Amen. Come, Lord Jesus. Despite all I have failed, You won't forget me. I don't need to cower in the back row on Judgment Day. When You bring Your kingdom, may I come too!"

Pray even when IT SEEMS THAT GOD IS PASSING YOU BY.

The blind beggar heard that Jesus was passing by, but he couldn't follow after Him. His one chance of healing was getting away! So he shouted out with a voice annoying to many but welcomed by Jesus (Mark 10:46–52). In these Second and Third Petitions of the Lord's Prayer, the kingdom of God is on the move, spanning heaven and earth. But what if He passes us by, blind beggars that we are? Don't despair and don't imagine that He and His kingdom come only to those who keep perfect pace with Him. Cry out with nothing more than, "Have mercy on me." This was the simple call that Jesus stopped to hear then and still hears now.

Tell Me More about Our Home

Remember camping in the rain? I hope you've experienced an epic three-day tent camping trip with your family, where by day three it had rained for forty-eight hours, the temperature had dropped to the mid-40s, a carpet of sandy grit covered every inch of the tent floor, and the ice in the chest had melted—the milk no longer as cold as it should be. How's the family feeling now? You can hear the groaning and their one question, "Why don't we go home?" We do have a home to go to. By the morning of the third day, we wonder why we ever left it. Sitting in the rainy woods in a soaked tent, we can't imagine leaving warm beds, full refrigerators, and 567 channels of cable TV ever again.

Now imagine someone who goes camping like this for the first time. Stretch my story to allow that this is a child being adopted into the family, picked up at an airport by his new family, and taken not home, but camping. For three days, the family camps and the rain falls. The family is tired, hungry, and grumpy. The child, just adopted, has to wonder, "Is this how life with these people is going to be? This tent is their home? This is their only food? This is how they get along? This is as good as it's going to get? Take me back to the foster home!" Then his brother hears him worrying that this family will always live in a tent in the woods. His brother laughs and says, "Don't you know? This is a tent. We have a house. This is just camping. Did you think this was all that Dad could do? Wait until we get home!"

I wonder if we often pray like that adopted child. We might think that this earth, with its problems raining down on us, is the best our Father can do. We might gauge the glory, the power, and the kingship of our God by the leaky tent we're living in today. Hearing these thoughts, the angels need to clap us on the shoulder, laughing, and say, "Look up. This body of yours is but a tent, and this life is just camping. But you're going home. Don't think that this is all your Father can do. Ask Him. Ask Him to make more of this time on earth like heaven. But don't forget. There is so much more to come. This is only camping. You're going home soon."

As we pray, "Thy kingdom come, Thy will be done on earth as it is in heaven," remember that we are only camping here. As Paul reminds us in 2 Corinthians 5:1–2, we are now living in our bodies as in a tent, "for we know that if the tent that is our earthly home is destroyed, we have a building from God, a house not made with hands, eternal in the heavens. For in this tent, we groan, longing to put on our heavenly dwelling." An eternal, perfected home is waiting for us. Don't imagine that this failing earth is the best God can do, or that His children can't hope to get along with one another better than we do now. We are children camping far to the east of Eden. Of course, we're often sharp with one another, and of course, this often-torn tent of our bodies isn't everything that our Father can do for us.

Our prayer is that we would not despair, but rather be assured that the perfect home in heaven will come. Return to my earlier story about the adopted child. If he believes his new brother's assurance

I know we're not home yet, but can't we act like we are?

that this is only camping and a proper house is waiting for them, what would you expect him to do? Wouldn't he begin to ask, "So what's it like there? What do we do? What do we eat? How do we get along?" I imagine that he would devour the family's stories of a full refrigerator, favorite meals, dry beds, and 567 channels of cable TV. He might hear that, at home, they really don't fight at all. In fact, they're not at all like they are in this wet tent. He'd say, "Can't we live like that already? I know we're not home yet, but can't we act like we are? If we can't watch TV, tell me what it'll be like when we do. If we can't cook every meal just like at home, couldn't we at least make the pancakes? Even though we're tired and wet, couldn't we at least say, 'I love you?'"

In our prayers, we need the view of an eager child looking past this camping trip to the home he's not yet seen. We need the restlessness of a child taking his father's hand and saying, "I know this isn't where we're always going to live, but couldn't we make it more like the home that's going to come? Won't you come and show us how it's going to be?" We ask that our Father would hurry His kingdom and His will so that they'll shape the way that we live today. We know that His kingdom and will are done of themselves and will come according to His own time, just as the boy knows that someday his family is going to leave the tent and go home. But like the boy, we want to have something of that home already.

What does that look like? Luther summarizes the prayer for the kingdom of God by saying,

"Dear Father, we pray, give us first Your Word, so that the Gospel may be preached properly throughout the world. Second, may the Gospel be received in faith and work and live in us. . . . And we pray that the devil's kingdom be put down [Luke 11:17–20], so that he may have no right or power over us [Luke 10:17–19; Colossians 1]. . . . Then we may live forever in perfect righteousness and blessedness" [Ephesians 4:12–13]. (Large Catechism, Part III, paragraph 54)

We're asking that God's kingdom and will come quickly and that they show their presence already.

In daily living, perhaps it is a combination of the many images that we have used in this chapter. In these two petitions, we make many steps on that slope leading from heaven to earth. Picture the different images we've drawn: the farmer who takes us along to do chores, the Master Carpenter who goes home with us, the killdeer on their trusting walk, and the family camping three days in the rain while a dry home is waiting for them. Each is a step toward earth.

We ask our Father to come with us as we, like eager children, set out into the world. *"You come too, Father, to help us see Your kingdom and will as they are already here."*

As we continue hallowing His name in heaven, we're ready to turn our river of praise into useful work, knowing that this river is unstoppable despite the obstacles and forces arranged against it. *"Father, make us useful servants in Your kingdom, working with Your heavenly power."*

We're asking that we would be noticed in His kingdom when it comes because we know this kingdom comes with incredible grace that welcomes the worst. *"Father, remember me in Your kingdom."*

Finally, we're newly adopted children, asking that even while we're far from our final home, we would be taught how to live as though we were already home. *"Father, until we finally get home, help us to live as Your hopeful children, doing Your will."*

In all, we wish the Father would come with us to the world that's waiting. We would rather not leave heaven at all, but if we must, it won't be for long. *"Father, you come too."*

CHAPTER FOUR

{ Showers When They Come }

IN THE SUMMER OF 1976, WEST CENTRAL MINNESOTA HAD A TERRIBLE DROUGHT. Our dairy farm had virtually no rain for over two months from June through August. The hay gave one poor cutting in June and never grew after that. The oats crop was so thin, we didn't waste fuel on harvesting it. And since we couldn't harvest enough hay or feed for our herd for the winter, we had to truck it in from Canada. On June 7 of the next year, we sold our entire dairy herd.

I remember that summer for many reasons. The scorched earth cracked open in jagged lines, looking like a lightning strike that had grounded itself. Real lightning came often at night. I listened to the thunder and our windows rattling and prayed that it would rain. But it didn't. Eventually, we would see clouds come, but our defeated response became, "It won't rain." For a long time, we were right. The drought was killing a year's worth of work. We watched the weather and tracked every cloud, but what difference did it make?

That's the final memory that is still strong after all these years. What could we do? We stood in the yard and watched the sky. We wondered if it would ever rain again. It was as if the clouds had completely forgotten how to rain. What I wanted to hear was rain on the metal roof of our machine shed, a few drops *Nothing makes us ready for the Fourth Petition of the Lord's Prayer like standing under an empty heaven, wondering if the rain's ever going to come.* first and then a pounding flood. That summer of 1976, I was ready to stand in the middle of the yard and get completely soaked. Our fields aside, my personal rain gauge was empty, and I needed filling.

Have you wondered whether heaven has forgotten to rain on you? Maybe it's been a drought for you lately. Your drought hasn't been on the news, no disaster funds are coming your way, and your closest friends are doing fine. But you've stood under heaven looking, waiting, and praying that the rain you need would come. You've seen clouds approach, but you have this feeling that, once again, they won't rain on you. Hope fights with despair. Maybe heaven has finally forgotten how to bring that rain cloud over you.

I hope you've had a dry summer. Nothing makes us ready for the Fourth Petition of the Lord's Prayer like standing under an empty heaven, wondering if the rain's ever going to come. This petition seems to be all about earth, but it's really about heaven too. We've been in our Father's heavenly home, joined in His praising choir, and we've taken His hand to bring His kingdom and will with us here. Now we're firmly on earth, but looking up to heaven. Our daily bread is the rain that God pours over us in His way and in His time. So we pray that He would send enough, at least for today. We want Him to stand here with us while we wait. Our journey may have left heaven in a way, but bread comes from heaven just as rain comes from its clouds. "Lord, let us stand with You in the open, look up, ask for heaven to open, and trust that it will with You."

> *Bread binds us to heaven as much as singing in heaven's choir and taking our Father's hand.*

In our diagram of the prayer, we're in the middle ground now. It's possible to see only the distance from heaven and the remarkable change that occurs with the Fourth Petition. We've left the three petitions focused on God's name, kingdom, and will. In the Greek text of Matthew 6:9–10, each of these three clauses begins with a verb and ends with the pronoun "your." In the Greek, the Fourth Petition begins sharply with "our bread." We may imagine that the prayer has taken a sharp turn, left heavenly things, and is either gladly or grudgingly focused on bread now. But in our journey through the prayer, we see that we are always connected with heaven. Daily bread is the rain from heaven that sometimes we wait for, standing in a dry yard looking up. When it finally comes, we still look up as it covers us. Bread binds us to heaven as much as singing in heaven's choir and taking our Father's hand.

HEAVEN   HEAVEN

OUR FATHER   KINGDOM
—NAME   & POWER

KINGDOM COME   DELIVER US

WILL BE DONE   LEAD US NOT

DAILY BREAD   FORGIVENESS

EARTH

I Would Ride the Clouds If I Could

When the drought came in '76, I wanted to be in charge of the clouds. We'd see clouds come up in the west and sometimes even see the thinnest rain coming from them. But day after day, those clouds would veer north or south, missing us. We knew there was rain in those clouds. If only we could steer them our way and have them unload on us.

When we come to the Fourth Petition, we probably want to ride the clouds. We'd like to load them with everything we want and send them directly over our house. Then we'd pull the cord and let the gifts fall, like a heavenly piñata funneled right over us. Given a chance, we'd tell God exactly what gifts we want and when they should arrive. It would be good to be in charge and to order up a week's supply of bread and have it delivered all today. Stock up the freezer, fill the shelves, let the counters overflow. Pour the bread of heaven on us.

But heavenly bread refuses to come on demand—on our demand. The analogy of bread that falls like rain has likely been reminding you of the manna that sustained Israel for the forty years they wandered in the wilderness. The story of the manna's introduction to Israel (Exodus 16) has many of our feelings toward daily bread. The people remember fondly their former food, even though it was the food of slavery. They were sure that they were being left to starve in a cloudless desert. God promised manna each morning, but only enough for that day. Despite being promised that tomorrow's bread would come, some were fearful and gathered enough for the next day also. It rotted. Heavenly bread comes like each morning's dew or a shower sufficient just for that day. There is no flood of food and no storing up.

Pray even when
GOD HAS SAID NO.

King Hezekiah was dying. Isaiah told him that he would not recover. It was clear that God had spoken. But Hezekiah prayed and God said, "I have heard your prayer; I have seen your tears" (Isaiah 38:5). Fifteen more years were given to Hezekiah (38:1–5). When the skies above us are empty and the cracks in the ground print out "NO," pray. Pray even if it seems that God has said no. Simple words of asking can fill the empty sky and reach a waiting Father.

When we pray the Lord's Prayer, we are people waiting for heavenly bread. Despite our desire to ride the clouds and situate them over our homes, the Lord's Prayer puts us back on earth looking to heaven. The difference, however, between my watching in '76 and my praying today is one of faith. In '76, we didn't expect it to rain. We painted buildings even when clouds were gathering. We dared it to rain on our freshly painted walls. "It won't rain," we said, and we were right.

But "Give us this day our daily bread" trusts that enough bread will come, at least for today. The idea of daily bread rests on the unusual word for "daily" used in both Matthew 6:11 and Luke 11:3 in this petition. The Greek word ἐπιούσιος, *epiousios*, is used only in these two verses. It has a variety of possible meanings with four being most likely: the bread necessary for existence, bread for today, bread for tomorrow, and bread for the coming Kingdom. No clear consensus exists for a single meaning. It seems likely that a combined meaning of "necessary" and "for today" is permissible and perhaps even intended.

Certainly these two are complementary to each other. The daily, absolutely necessary manna that fed Israel for forty years in the desert is an example of both of these understandings. Included in the bread is everything that pertains to our life, including our food and its fields, our houses and harmony within them, our work and the health to do it.[17] All of these are necessary and pertain to today and tomorrow. The illustration of manna perhaps allows the combination of today and tomorrow since on the eve of the Sabbath one was to gather twice as much as on any other day. Therefore, for those gathering bread from heaven, there is both a tending of the work for today and an eye for tomorrow.

This bread comes in a measure that fits today. At the writing of this book, it was being reported that the Houston area received over thirty inches of rain in the previous six days. Massive flooding resulted, of course. In the Milwaukee area where we live, it was noted that thirty inches of rain is almost all that we normally receive in a whole year. That's the point of God's gift of daily bread. Left to our driving of the clouds, we would probably unload upon ourselves a year's worth of bread in a week. While we're often frustrated with waiting for God's gifts, wondering why God hasn't come more quickly with a larger measure of blessing over us, we would certainly do worse for ourselves if we drove the clouds. I suspect that we would unleash far too much of all that is good.

In contrast, Proverbs 30:8–9 sums up the necessary balance: "Give me neither poverty nor riches; feed me with the food that is needful for me, lest I be full and deny you and say, 'Who is the LORD?'

---

17 Perhaps most comprehensive of the summaries that might be quoted in this regard is Luther's: "With many words one could list all the things that are included, like when we ask God to give us food and drink, clothing, house and home, and health of body. Or when we ask that He cause the grain and fruit of the field to grow and mature well. Furthermore, we ask that He help us at home with good housekeeping and that He give and preserve for us a godly wife, children, and servants. We ask that He cause our work, trade, or whatever we are engaged in to prosper and succeed, favor us with faithful neighbors and good friends, and other such things. Likewise, we ask that He give wisdom, strength, and success to emperors, kings, and all estates, and especially to the rulers of our country and to all counselors, magistrates, and officers. Then they may govern well and vanquish the Turks and all enemies. We ask that He give to subjects and the common people obedience, peace, and harmony in their life with one another. On the other hand, we ask that He would preserve us from all sorts of disaster to body and livelihood, like lightning, hail, fire, flood, poison, plague, cattle disease, war and bloodshed, famine, destructive beasts, wicked men, and so forth" (Large Catechism, Part III, paragraphs 76–78).

or lest I be poor and steal and profane the name of my God." Rather than railing beneath the clouds of heaven, we might adopt the attitude of David in Psalm 131:1–3: "I do not occupy myself with things too great and too marvelous for me. But I have calmed and quieted my soul, like a weaned child with its mother; like a weaned child is my soul within me. O Israel, hope in the LORD from this time forth and forevermore."

In one way, I wish I had been younger when the drought came to our farm. It would have been an easier time if I had been five instead of twenty. My parents could have said, "Don't worry. It'll be all right, whether it rains or not," and I probably would have believed them. Nonetheless, they were right. We never went hungry that year. Our lives changed, but they certainly went on. I couldn't drive the clouds, but the One who does brought them around in the end. The rain came back, the cracked earth healed, and crops grew the next year. Heaven hadn't forgotten how to rain on us.

The View from the Clouds

Farmers worry. They worry perhaps more than any group of people I've met. They worry first and foremost about the weather, though the prices of crops and livestock come in a close second. They watch every day's weather and can always tell you whether we need more rain or more sun, more wind or more calm. I doubt if visitors to a farm ever see the problems. The crops are in the fields with their various shades of green, the machinery is in the sheds waiting to go to work. The farmer seems to have this free time to stop whatever he's doing and to visit over coffee. I suspect that many a summertime visitor to a farm has said, "What a great life. I wish I could be a farmer."

Perhaps we see Him as only visiting from a floating, distant cloud, a city visitor pointing out wildflowers to a farmer who's been busy pulling weeds.

While the farmer is smiling over coffee, he's watching the clouds in the west. He's checking the clock to see if he can squeeze in making the hay before milking. He's wondering if that baler he didn't have time to fix will hold up for just a few more rounds today. Most visitors never notice the clouds, the clock, or the creaking baler.

Perhaps we should all visit one another's lives rather than live out our own. We might worry less if we were to only visit farms, not run them. Farmers visiting factories and offices and stores in the mall wouldn't worry over deadlines, overdue shipments, falling sales, and layoffs. If each of us merely visited one another's lives, we might have a detachment that would take in only the best points. It would be the view from the clouds. We would float over one another's lives, say encouraging things, point out how wonderful some part of this or that life is, and float away. It would be easy to view one another from a visiting cloud.

GROW IN THE GROUND THAT YOU HAVE

"A tranquil heart gives life to the flesh, but envy makes the bones rot" (Proverbs 14:30). Your neighbor's garden and lawn are bigger than yours and her flowers bloom more brightly. Grow enough envy and you'll stop planting your ground altogether. But as you wait like dry ground for God's shower of blessing, work the garden you've been given. Ask not for bigger fields but for greater contentment in the field you have. Lord, give me a tranquil heart that finds joy in the field in which You placed me.

I worry that is how we view God's visit and His rain of daily bread in the Fourth Petition. Perhaps we see Him as only visiting from a floating, distant cloud, a city visitor pointing out wildflowers to a farmer who's been busy pulling weeds. God could sail over us with a visitor's detachment and see our lives as more beautiful than we do. True, the farmer admits, there are flowers there. But, the farmer points out, the visitor missed seeing the Canadian thistle and the wild oats creeping into the fields. Most of our lives concentrate on weed watching. Even if the weeds haven't come into our fields yet, we know they're lurking.

But God could stay above all that. The sunny side of heaven's clouds echo the chorus of angels and praising saints. He could remind us in the Lord's Prayer to focus on His coming kingdom. He could breezily assure us that He'll feed us, and then say, "Don't worry so much about your life." We might hear God say only, "I feed the birds; I'll feed you. Now stop worrying." All that's true. Jesus reassures us that all the things we pursue, these our Father already knows we need (Matthew 6:32–33).

If that were all God said, who would blame Him? We would like to be so detached from our worries too. A life seated in the clouds with sunshine always on our faces would be fine. We could float over our own towns with the distance of a satellite picture. Then almost any place would look fine. Who wouldn't be content down there?

But God doesn't hover ten thousand feet above us. He doesn't see our personal, devastating droughts and simply say, "Don't worry. I'm sure they'll all work out." He isn't a casual summertime visitor who leaves without touching our lives. He is the one who questions that if you see a brother or sister without clothes or daily food and you say, "'Go in peace, be warm and filled,' without giving them the things needed for the body, what good is that?" (James 2:16). This God cannot merely say a brief word to us, have us call out for bread, and then deliver a stone or, worse, an airy clap on the back and a cheerful, "It'll all work out."

The way God delivers the bread is often like a summer shower. Look to the west and see the dark clouds building. Hear the muted rumble of thunder, though you missed any lightning. Look to the southwest and see the lines streaking down from that cloud. There's rain in those clouds, but they look like they'll sail over you. "Give us this day our daily bread" is said with an eye to the clouds of heaven that show they have rain for us in them. Oftentimes it's not raining yet. Heaven's bread doesn't fall on us like water from a sprinkler, ready any moment we want it to fall. It comes in its time. But take a look to the west. There's water in those clouds, and they're heading toward you.

That certainty fits especially well with the context of the Lord's Prayer in Luke 11:5–8. After Jesus finishes the prayer, He immediately tells the parable of the friend at midnight: A man pounds on his friend's door, asking for bread, and at first the friend says he can't get up to give anything. But after the man's shameless and continuous pounding and pleading, the friend finally gets up and gives the man what he is requesting. It's interesting that this is the vital point repeated for Luke's context. He doesn't return to the glory of heaven, the praise of His name, or even forgiveness as is the case with Matthew's context. The necessity of bread and the boldness of asking for it are the keys for

Luke's rendering of the prayer. One of the vital points for this parable of the friend at midnight is the man's certainty that there is bread in that house. The argument from inside the house is not "I don't have any bread." Everyone in the parable knows there's bread there. The point is to ask until it comes to you.

And so Jesus tells this prayer and parable to conclude, "And I tell you, ask, and it will be given to you; seek, and you will find; knock, and it will be opened to you" (Luke 11:9). There is bread and more in those heavenly clouds. We can see the streaks of rain coming down already in the promises God makes about prayer. Everything needed is in the cloud that promises daily bread.

In the Fourth Petition, God sums up His knowledge of our needs and His care for them. He promises, "I know all that you need, and I care even more than you do." Luther describes this knowledge powerfully and also describes the reason God commands us to pray when He already knows what we need:

> The reason He commands it is, of course, not in order
> to have us make our prayers an instruction to Him as
> to what He ought to give us, but in order to have us
> acknowledge and confess that He is already bestowing
> many blessings upon us and that He can and will give us
> still more. By our praying, therefore, we are instructing
> ourselves more than we are Him.[18]

His teaching through prayer lets us see a wider world under His care. Most of our worries center on how we are affected by what is happening. I cared about the dying crops in 1976 because of what they cost me. But God promises an even greater level of care. "I care not only for you because the crops are dying. I care for the dying crops themselves. The brittle corn and the barren stalk of oats are more to me than wasted seed. They're my own creation." God makes the same promise over your needs. The joy of praying to our Father is that He has an even greater attachment than we do to every event, person, animal, and plant about which we pray.

One of the best illustrations of this might be the remarkable miracle of Jesus feeding the five thousand. Isn't it a wonder that of all the

18 LW 21:144.

miracles He did, this is the only miracle recorded in all four Gospels? We might expect one of the resurrection miracles to be in every Gospel, but the raising of Lazarus is only in John 11, the raising of the son of the widow of Nain is only in Luke 7, and the raising of Jairus's daughter is in Matthew 9, Mark 5, and Luke 8. Yet, none of them commands the attention like the feeding of the five thousand and its essential repetition in the feeding of the four thousand. There is a central message about the care and ministry of Jesus when this becomes the miracle that is told over and over.

What is especially important to note is how easily Jesus could have avoided the entire situation. He and the disciples were themselves tired and hungry before the crowd ever came to them (Mark 6:31). By the end of the day, after listening to Jesus' teaching, the crowd was equally hungry. The disciples wanted to get back to the original plan of escaping the crowd and so urged Jesus to send the people away. How easily Jesus could have said, "You're right. I've fed them already with the best news they'll ever hear." But He says instead the words that the crowds must have cherished: "You give them something to eat" (Mark 6:37). When we hear that still today, we have new confidence when we pray the Fourth Petition and ask for our daily bread.

Your requests don't echo across a dry, mocking heaven. The Son Himself carries them to the Father, who knows what you need.

How easily the Father could listen to us pounding on the door at midnight and our repeated requests for bread and respond, "I've already fed you. I listened to you in the court of heaven, and I promised that My kingdom would come and include you. That's enough." But Jesus is more than that for us. He is an advocate who speaks to the Father on our behalf (Romans 8:34; Hebrews 9:24). As you pound on the midnight door, you hear a voice within say, "Give him something to eat." You can already hear the approaching thunder of rain coming to your thirsty place and the echo of those heavenly words, "Give them something to eat." The Father is already inclined to give us the bread we need. But urging on our prayers and the confidence with which we ask is the Son. "He is able to save to the uttermost [that is, "completely" or "at all times"] those who draw near to God through

Him, since He always lives to make intercession for them" (Hebrews 7:25). Let His trademark miracle and His own words to the disciples be your assurance when you pray.

This is part of why we pray. We pray, but not to pull God into doing what He doesn't want to do. We pray not just to see Him do what He would have done regardless. And we pray not to hear only our words. We pray to hear the words that are said for us by Christ. We ask for bread so that we can hear Him second our request and say, "Give them something to eat." We pray as Martin Chemnitz said, "In our prayers we lay our wants and needs before God, not as though He did not know them, but that by pouring out our cares into the Lord's bosom, we may unburden and comfort our souls. . . . Chrysostom adds this reason why we should pray: 'That by often calling upon God we may become familiar with Him.'"[19] Take heart. Your requests don't echo across a dry, mocking heaven. The Son Himself carries them to the Father, who knows what you need. There's rain in those clouds for you, and the One who drives the clouds is telling them, "You give them something to eat."

Who Would Ever Choose a Drought?

But if God rides over the clouds and orders them where He wants, and if He wants His own to be fed, why is there ever a drought? And why do droughts come in so many ways? First, you suffer through a drought of health, then later come the unending worries about your children. At one time their futures were full and promising, but now they're drying up. Has the world slipped beyond the Father's control so that, though He would help, He cannot? Or are these problems all so little that, with His view from the clouds, He doesn't worry about them? Is God too farsighted, too globally minded to see me?

I can only suggest silencing this mystery with one that is greater: why would a loving Father choose these droughts for His children? I don't have an answer that's quick and satisfying. One that is quick is probably too simple. One that will satisfy would require more volumes than anyone has written. I suspect that on this side of life no one will ever write all the answers to our mysteries. But there may be a solution, at least as much as we might have here, in answering a mystery with a

---

19 Martin Chemnitz, *Ministry, Word, and Sacraments: An Enchiridion*, trans. Luther Poellot, J. A. O. Preus, and Georg Williams (St. Louis: Concordia, 2007), 14.

mystery. Why would anyone choose a drought for his children? Answer that with this question: What is the depth of the heavenly Father's love for mankind that He would send a His perfect Son into drought and death? Sending Jesus into the drought of our experience, to be parched and die, is a mystery greater than our own bitter experience.

This is a pair of mysteries put together. On one hand, we can see meal after meal that Jesus missed, leaving Him hungry or thirsty. On the other, the One who is hungry calls Himself bread. Isn't it ironic that He is the water of life to the woman at the Samaritan well, the very woman whom He asks for a drink? He identifies Himself as the bread of life in John 6 to those whom He fed with a few loaves and fish. Yet, the day in which He fed them, He and His own disciples had little time for eating and were in need of a retreat.

Think of the droughts Jesus experienced that overshadow our own lack. He began His ministry in the joyous water of Baptism in the Jordan. But then, as the benevolent cloud of the Father's praise was fading, "the Spirit immediately drove Him out into the wilderness. And He was in the wilderness forty days, being tempted by Satan" (Mark 1:12–13). In the desert, He was hungry and was tempted by stones waiting to be turned into bread. Yet, He refused to end His fast on Satan's terms.

It's this hungry love that made Him feed the five thousand.

While His ministry begins in this refusal of bread, Jesus ends His time with the twelve disciples with the bread of the Lord's Supper. In His closing moments with the disciples, He could use any part of His creation. He could have defined His ministry and His bond with the disciples with piercing light, dancing flame, or rock-splitting wind. But He chose bread and wine. Further, it is in the breaking of the bread in Luke 24 that He is later recognized by the Emmaus road disciples. He does more than supply bread; He defines Himself with this bread.

Yet, less than twenty-four hours after the Last Supper, He is dying, thirsty, on a cross. The One who pours out wine (and thereby His blood) and invites others to drink of it must say, when words are few and dear, "I thirst" (John 19:28). They reached to Him with a sponge of sour wine and He took a drink. In John's Gospel, that is His final act before He says, "It is finished." He thirsted, drank, and died. No matter how dry we've been, we've never thirsted like that. We may stand under a cloudless heaven and wonder if it's forgotten to rain, but have we thirsted to death?

The tempter still intrudes when I'm praying and asks, "If you were really the child of God, wouldn't He just give you the bread you ask for without making you wait or saying no? What kind of father would make you endure this agonizing drought? He promised you more than this. But look, all you have is dry ground. You're no child of His, and He's no father to you."

I could answer this with the promises of God to feed His children. Elijah and the widow were sustained in the drought with miraculous bread (1 Kings 17:7–16). Israel was fed for forty monotonous years (Exodus 16:35). All of this is true and answers the question to a point. But for me, the better answer is to match mystery with mystery. Better to challenge the tempter. Say, "You're right, at least as far as I can see. God should be feeding me more. But He isn't right now, at least that is as much as I know. But answer me this: Why did He go hungry Himself? He became a man, but why become a hungry one? And admit it, He was really hungry. That's why you tempted Him. If He were selfish, He would have fed Himself. If He were weak and couldn't have turned the stones to bread, you would never have tempted Him. So why didn't He turn them into bread? He's a hungry man with the power of God. Why not feed Himself?"

What can the tempter say? He can't say that he doesn't have an answer. That leaves him no better than I am. He can't suggest that God will get something out of His hunger. He's already God. What will hunger bring Him? But what Satan especially will not say is that Christ went hungry for me. Satan can't say that God loves me so much that His love left Him hungry. It's this love that sent Him from the clouds in the first place. It's this hungry love that made Him feed the five thousand. Satan won't admit this. Christ went hungry because of His love for the world. If Satan ever dares to admit that, then we'll talk about the drought I feel today.

One mystery might overwhelm another. Perhaps in heaven, the timing of the droughts of our lives will all come clear as we see them from the clouds of heaven. We'll see a pattern that we missed from the ground. But for now, there's this. More than an airy "Don't worry, it'll work out," we have these words for our droughts: "He went hungry too.

He was thirsty, even to the point of death. The ground cracked open and took Him in. He did it because He loves you."

Waiting for the Clouds

As we close this petition, perhaps this could be our prayer: "Rain this day our daily bread. Let us never forget the heaven from which it comes and the hand that brings it here. Give us patience when the sky is empty. Give us thanks when the showers fall. Don't let us spoil Your gifts by asking, 'Is this all?' Let the only wonder in our waiting be this: 'Why would You ever go hungry for me? Why would You be thirsty enough to die?'"

I hope that the droughts you face turn your eyes up to heaven. The Fourth Petition plants our feet on earth but brings our words and hopes to heaven. Though this petition seems the simplest, asking only for bread, it reminds us of the deepest mystery. God becomes man, and the Father leaves His Son hungry. When our bread is delayed, remember His hunger. When our bread comes, remember His love. The showers will come in His time.

CHAPTER FIVE

{ The Flood }

HAVE YOU EVER BEEN IN A FLOOD? Has water bullied its way through community levees, overrun your sandbag dikes, rushed up to your home, and overwhelmed your sump pump? Have you stood outside your house, hip-deep in water, and watched boats go up your street?

In June 1997, our house flooded. A week's worth of rain was capped off with six inches overnight. Our street was overwhelmed. Soon water was pooling around several houses, including ours. The water covered the yard and came up to the bottom of the basement windows. Our house became one of many "islands" in the neighborhood. There was a foot of water in the basement, and the level was rising. The fire department brought in a gas-powered pump, rowing it up the street in a red canoe. Once the pump was in our basement, its discharge hose snaked its way up the basement steps, went through the garage, and was propped up in the yard where it shot brown water back into the flood.

In the Fifth Petition, we come to God's flood. Forgiveness pours out on us beyond any reasonable measure.

In the middle of all this, three of us neighbors just stood in the street. The rain was still pouring down, the water was rising, and the fire department's hose, like a water cannon, was roaring away behind us. In the street, we were in water above our knees. I have never been in the midst of so much water. It was pushing its way into every crack of our lives. We could pump it out, but it seemed to come back even more.

Imagine if in the middle of this scene, one of our neighbors whose property was a bit higher and not flooded had come to me and asked,

"Say, could you spare a little water? I was hoping I could have some from that fire hose or maybe a little from your backyard. I wouldn't take it all—just a little." What would I say? "No, sorry, I think I better hold on to it. I was just thinking of building a dike to hold it in. That way we wouldn't have to mow the lawn anymore. Sorry, but I don't really have much to spare." If I had said anything that ridiculous, it would have been clear that I had breathed too many exhaust fumes from the pump running in our basement.

If that man had actually asked for water, I might wonder if he was serious. But I wouldn't ask too many questions. "Water? You want water? Take it! We're going under. You can take all you want. Fire up a pump and roll out a hose. I've got water, and you can have it!"

In the Fifth Petition, we come to God's flood. Forgiveness pours out on us beyond any reasonable measure. It's a perfect flood that covers us, infiltrates our lives, and overwhelms the boundaries we have among ourselves. It comes with such abundance that our neighbors can have any amount they wish from us. "And forgive us our trespasses as we forgive those who trespass against us." In this flood of forgiveness, any refusal would be unthinkable. The flood of forgiveness ties us to heaven in the most benevolent way and gives an immediacy to the gifts of God. In this chapter, we'll expand on this central idea of the overflow of forgiveness, which binds us to heaven and pours out to those near us.

Finally, No Waiting

With the petition for daily bread, we are waiting on dry ground for a rain that has not fully come—at least not yet. We look up from dry earth to the coming clouds and trust that the Lord of heaven knows what we need on earth. We want to be done with waiting for His gifts. Even when daily bread does come, there's *At the heart of the prayer is the Fifth Petition, because the source of hope for all the other petitions is this: we are forgiven.* still a degree of waiting involved. There's a ration, a daily bread diet. There's only so much in each day's allowance. But our Father assures us that His gifts come with the right measure.

But with the Fifth Petition, we have a request that doesn't require us to wait. Here is an overflow such that any amount we might ask is already given. We experience no delay since the flood of forgiveness is already pressing upon our door and seeping into every part of our lives. We might be sleeping through it, just as many a flood comes at night while we're unaware. So this flood of forgiveness has already come, and it's time to wake up to it.

Pray even when ALL YOU CAN SAY IS, "HAVE MERCY."

The tax collector praying in the temple had nothing to say, no boasts to compare with the Pharisee who went ahead of him. With no excuses or promises, his prayer had no beauty to be heard. He said only "God, be merciful to me, a sinner!" Yet, this man went home justified with God (Luke 18:9–14). When you have nothing to say over all that has been done, call out for mercy. Mercy needs no long invitation—even barely mumbled, our words reach the heart of God's mercy.

There is no waiting for this forgiveness. Second Corinthians 5:19 showers this gift upon us, saying, "In Christ God was reconciling the world to Himself, not counting their trespasses against them." This benevolent flood from heaven covers the entire world, and no mountain of sin escapes it. Paul's past mountain of sin was as high as anyone's, yet he's certain that he's covered by God's flood of forgiveness:

The saying is trustworthy and deserving of full acceptance, that Christ Jesus came into the world to save sinners, of whom I am the foremost. But I received mercy for this reason, that in me, as the foremost, Jesus Christ might display His perfect patience as an example to those who were to believe in Him for eternal life. (1 Timothy 1:15–16)

In this flood of forgiveness, we are all on the same perfectly level plane. The saving forgiveness floods over us with the immediacy of water, which never waits.

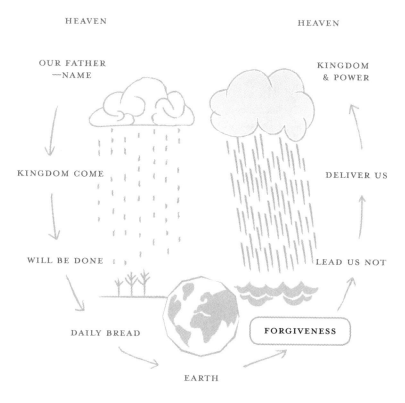

HEAVEN   HEAVEN

OUR FATHER   KINGDOM
—NAME   & POWER

KINGDOM COME   DELIVER US

WILL BE DONE   LEAD US NOT

DAILY BREAD   FORGIVENESS

EARTH

In our other petitions, we wait for some aspect of the prayer to be fully done. We speak of the perfect holiness of God's name, but often there is no echo of this perfect name in a world of curses. We look for His kingdom to arrive completely, but all we might see today are vain kings whose kingdoms are still at war. We stand in dry yards, waiting for the clouds to feed us. But here is forgiveness lapping at our doorstep and creeping up our windows. Every morning, the first sound we hear could be the splashing of forgiveness against our house. Those who come to us have to wade through it; we should be able to hear them as they walk through a moat of forgiveness to arrive at us. Forgiveness wants to cover us like a six-inch rain.

Isn't this immediacy a remarkable offer and a refreshing change in our prayer? It is astonishing because forgiveness is all because of His sacrifice alone. However, if we were forgiven in any way due to our own work, then this petition could easily have been put last in the Lord's Prayer. Forgiveness would be a spiritual mountaintop that no one could reach. If we were forgiven in any way by ourselves, then forgiveness would be a spiritual marathon that no one ever finished.

However, Luther points out that forgiveness is the essential quality needed for prayer to begin: "For where the heart is not in a right relationship with God, or cannot take such confidence, it will not dare to pray anymore. Such a confident and joyful heart can spring from nothing else than the certain knowledge of the forgiveness of sin" *If God will feed us, then He will forgive. He wouldn't feed us just to condemn us. He wouldn't encourage us and then crush us.* (Large Catechism, Part III, paragraph 92). If we are forgiven, then we can hallow and praise His name. We can welcome His kingdom and will because we know we have a place in it. We're sure of His feeding because we are those He died to forgive. We'll be protected from the evil one and delivered to heaven because of forgiveness. At the heart of the prayer is the Fifth Petition, because the source of hope for all the other petitions is this: we are forgiven.

If forgiveness is the foundation for prayer, then why does it come after asking for daily bread? In a sense of importance, forgiveness has the greater, eternal weight. Wouldn't it be more sensible that forgiveness should precede bread? However, there are at least two reasons that give a rationale for the order of the prayer. First, the prayer for bread recognizes our nearly automatic human concern for the physical necessities of life, coupled with a wider understanding of Jesus as the bread of life and the giver of bread that is His body. Our asking for bread is not necessarily selfish grasping. It's a natural concern for the food that God is eager to give and which speaks about God's own nature. Second, if the greater issue with God is forgiveness and the relationship one has with the Father, bread is a fitting beginning. If God will feed us, then He will forgive. He wouldn't feed us just to condemn us. He wouldn't encourage us and then crush us. He feeds us because He has forgiven and will forgive again. With our analogy of the shower of daily bread and the flood of forgiveness, we stand in dry yards looking for the shower but do so on ground that has been washed over and renewed in the flood of forgiveness.

But this immediacy of forgiveness doesn't mean that all are automatically forgiven and no prayer for forgiveness is needed. We pray that God would draw us out of our ignorant sleep, lead us into this forgiveness, and let us be soaked through with forgiveness. The prayer doesn't create the forgiveness that has already come to the world. It doesn't make God decide to take us. This has happened already because "He chose us in Him before the foundation of the world, that we should be holy and blameless before Him" (Ephesians 1:4). Luther balances both the existence of forgiveness before we pray and our need to pray:

> It is not as though He did not forgive sin without and even before our prayer. (He has given us the Gospel, in which is pure forgiveness before we prayed or ever thought about it [Romans 5:8].) But the purpose of this prayer is that we may recognize and receive such forgiveness. The flesh in which we daily live is of such a nature that it neither trusts nor believes God [Romans 7:14–18]. . . . By this the conscience is thrown into unrest, so that it is afraid of God's wrath and displeasure. So it loses the comfort and confidence derived from the Gospel. Therefore, it is always necessary that we run here and receive consolation to comfort the conscience again. (Large Catechism, Part III, paragraphs 88–89)

Our prayer is that we would realize this forgiveness, much as we pray that the already hallowed name would be hallowed by us and that the coming kingdom would come among us. "Father, You feed the just and unjust and let us know that our daily gifts come from You. Lord, you forgive all the unjust; now reassure us that You forgive even us."

This prayer for forgiveness lifts our eyes upward to see the gift that is pouring over us. If we were not praying, we might imagine that forgiveness simply comes as a part of life, as automatic as a heartbeat. Or we might think that we have deserved it by our manner of living so that the real cause of the forgiveness is in ourselves. The image of the Lord's Prayer as a journey reminds us always of the connection with heaven. Heaven pours out the flood of forgiveness. It comes like one night's six-inch rain. So God has come with His abundance of forgiveness over us, choosing by His grace to cover us. We pray that we might wake up to this downpour and its eagerness to press into every crevice of our lives. Thankfully, there is no waiting for this flood; it has already come.

Covering the Tracks

The words of the prayer bring the sound of this forgiving flood. We pray and, by this, step into the flood. In this abundance of forgiveness, we notice how our plans change. When a flood covers your home, it demands all that you have; it creates a singular focus. The schedule you had for the day is washed away.

Forgiveness is a vigorous action that undoes the ordinary actions of a day. Like a flood, it takes precedent over everything else. On the day of our 1997 flood, our son, Steve, had an orthodontist appointment. Though I thought he should go, Holly wisely said no, the rain was too heavy and the streets were going under. I was to go to St. Louis the next day, but that trip was pushed back. No one had time for a regular meal until that night, and if anyone had planned to run errands or go shopping, they never mentioned it. The flood demanded all our attention.

Forgiveness is a heavenly, benevolent torrent that captures us. Like a proper flood, it hangs over us and is a mark that stays with us.

Forgiveness has that same demanding, all-consuming power. A flood of forgiveness sets new priorities for us. In a flood, we're suddenly appreciative of the basic things—our walls standing while a neighbor's basement starts to buckle, our own health when another neighbor is taken to the hospital. When the rain finally stopped and the sun came out, as it did that evening in 1997, we reveled in sunshine that otherwise we never would have noticed. Forgiveness is both flood and sunshine suddenly seen, the favor of God that we finally recognize.

Forgiveness is this flood that rushes up to demand our attention. Forgiveness needs the most powerful image. Perhaps a flood unearths very painful memories for you, or maybe your cleanup efforts are still ongoing. Or perhaps your only experience with a flood is watching one on the news. We could speak of being in a waterfall or standing under a jet of water at a water park, and they would certainly give us the feeling of water in abundance. But they lack the urgency of a flood and the connection with the clouds. Forgiveness is a heavenly, benevolent torrent that captures us. Like a proper flood, it hangs over us and is a mark that stays with us. Everyone who experienced the flood of '97 knows how high the water was, how many rows of cement blocks were covered in their basements. It was the topic of conversation for the rest of the summer, and every heavy rain since has been measured against the flood of '97.

Forgiveness is determined to be the same urgent centerpiece of our lives. It would be the mark that others notice about us. It could be the conversation that's started about us: "Their house was in the flood, you know. You can tell." Isn't that the way we want to be known in each of our towns? We're the house that's been engulfed in forgiveness. We want people to say: "Those people, they were in the forgiveness flood. You can tell. They've never been quite the same."

Forgiveness sets all the other business of the day aside and says, "First you attend to this. Then turn your attention to something else, if there is anything else." That very idea is the context of Matthew's rendering of the Lord's Prayer, where the two verses following the prayer repeat the need for forgiveness to be shared in order that it might be fully experienced (6:14–15). These closing words from Matthew's text of the Lord's Prayer say in essence, "If you are not forgiving, you're not forgiven. What hope is there, then, for all the other words of your prayer?"

But a flood makes for a wonderfully simple day also. Our concentration was focused entirely on the rising water in our basement and the high watermark on the outside walls of the house. No one fretted about the other seventy-three details of life. We didn't worry about how to hang the wallpaper we had just purchased or what we should make for supper or how Nicole's new swimming teacher was working out. It was water only that day. At the end of the day, when the basement had finally been pumped out and the water was receding from the streets, we went to sleep thankful for cool showers and dry beds.

Think of the simplicity of the Fifth Petition. "Forgive us, Lord, and that will be enough." Our cry in this petition is not so much "Give us what we don't have," for we have already seen the flood of His forgiveness. Instead, in asking for this forgiveness, we're saying, "Give us a mind that is content with this and nothing else." Isn't that a wonderful escape from the to-do list of your life? Isn't this a place to linger, just as we did with the praising of His name in the heavenly choir? Who wouldn't want to stay here a bit, asking for forgiveness that is already pressing in upon our lives and quieting all the other worries of life, at least for a time? For this moment in the prayer, we can say to the noisiest problem that continually tugs on our sleeve, "Don't bother me now. The floodwaters of forgiveness are rising all around me."

I suppose few of us go on a totally relaxing vacation where there is no stress, only complete relaxation. We might plan for that kind of vacation, but those plans seldom become reality. However, in the Fifth Petition, we have an enduring moment of peace for our souls. Here is a spa for the spirit. We're asking for what God has already provided in His Son and what He is pressing upon us even before we ask. Here is a request of such importance that it silences all the other demands of life. Lock the door of your mind for this moment and hang this sign on the outside: "Do not disturb. Forgiveness at work." Then be assured with the words of 1 John concerning this prayer for forgiveness above all the other gifts God is inclined to give us: "This is the confidence that we have toward Him, that if we ask anything according to His will He hears us. And if we know that He hears us in whatever we ask, we know that we have the requests that we have asked of Him" (5:14–15). When we ask for forgiveness, we are in the center of His will for us. At least for a moment, we have rest from our other work. If ever we've found what we're supposed to be doing, it's asking for, receiving, and giving forgiveness.

Covering Over the Lines

Now that we've found what we're supposed to be doing ourselves, it's time to turn to our neighbors. While being forgiven is, in one way, a luxurious retreat and a private moment with our Father, it also draws us into our neighbors' lives. That's the thing about a flood. It's vertical water only for a moment. In a heartbeat, those six inches of water spread out, and they cover far more than six inches of ground. So it is with forgiveness. It is an overwhelming covering for each of us, but it immediately spreads out to our neighbors and draws us with it.

In a flood, property lines mean very little. The water doesn't care where my grass ends and my neighbor's starts. When leaving mud, old cornstalks, or plastic children's toys on front lawns, the rain covers dandelions and marigolds all the same. Firemen march over your front room carpet carrying a pump still dripping from the water outside. Who cares about the carpet? We need this pump, and they're good to bring it. People wade through the water and our floating lawn furniture to go swimming in our backyard during the flood, and we laugh. The little girls next door blow up their pink air mattress and go sailing through the neighborhood. They sail right over our garden. But no one worried about trespassing. It's the middle of a flood.

In the flood of forgiveness, there is no worrying about trespassing either. The traditional liturgical wording of the Lord's Prayer, as found in *Lutheran Service Book*, brings out this idea when it reads, "Forgive us our *trespasses* as we forgive those who *trespass* against us" (emphasis added). Matthew 6:14, "For if you forgive others their trespasses," uses the Greek word παράπτωμα, *paraptoma*, meaning a missed step, transgression, or sin. Here, Jesus expands on the need for forgiving others. This sense was then transferred to the Lord's Prayer itself and is retained in many liturgical settings of the prayer. Luke uses another combination of words in the Fifth Petition: "Forgive us our sins, for we ourselves forgive everyone who is indebted to us" (Luke 11:4). The word for "sins" is the plural of ἁμαρτία, *hamartia*, the familiar word for sin, which can mean the actual deed, its result, and the power that causes the sin.

The idea of a trespass gives a vivid image to the act of forgiveness. We probably can trace every step made by the many who have trespassed on us. That's the thing about most sins. They leave a mark behind. A trail of broken twigs and scorched and blackened grass in our yards tell who trespassed against us. And we've left our own trail of distinct prints behind in our neighbors' and families' lives. Sometimes we're clueless wanderers, like children who simply play in whatever yard looks inviting. Far more often we know exactly where we are, though we hope that the grass will grow back, cover our footprints, and never tell on us. But looking back, our trail is still clear.

But forgiveness is a covering, washing flood. David cries for this cleansing in Psalm 51:2, 7: "Wash me thoroughly from my iniquity, and cleanse me from my sin! . . . Purge me with hyssop, and I shall be clean; wash me, and I shall be whiter than snow." He describes forgiveness as this cover in Psalm 32:1, "Blessed is the one whose transgression is forgiven, whose sin is covered." Under the water of forgiveness, there is no record left of our tracks. Our pasts are memories at most. This is the pattern when Paul writes to the Corinthians describing their former lives before their washing in forgiveness:

The washing blood of Christ is not crystal clear, but is blessedly opaque. We can't see through His blood as it covers the trespasses of the world.

> Do not be deceived: neither the sexually immoral, nor idolaters, nor adulterers, nor men who practice homosexuality, nor thieves, nor the greedy, nor drunkards, nor revilers, nor swindlers will inherit the kingdom of God. And such were some of you. But you were washed, you were sanctified, you were justified in the name of the Lord Jesus Christ and by the Spirit of our God. (1 Corinthians 6:9–11)

Forgiveness covers not only our tracks; it also covers our neighbor's. Forgiving your neighbor's trespasses is much easier when a flood covers both of your properties. Who can tell where anyone has been? Besides, it's likely that when he comes over to collect his children's wading pool and apologize for it ending up on your deck, you'll have to do the same for your lawn chairs that landed in his bushes. When the forgiveness of God sweeps over us, how can any of us see clearly the trespasses of our neighbors? They are lost somewhere beneath the water of our Baptism. The washing blood of Christ is not crystal clear, but rather blessedly opaque. We can't see through His blood as it covers the trespasses of the world. It's enough to know that the trespasses are lost beneath it. The washing of forgiveness finally lets us say, "What trespasses? They *were* here, but I just can't see them anymore." The simple words "Forgive us our trespasses as we forgive those who trespass against us" show us a dark flood that overruns the property lines and hides the marks we each have left behind.

GROW FLOWERS, NOT THORNS

"A soft answer turns away wrath, but a harsh word stirs up anger" (Proverbs 15:1). You can grow a prickly hedge around your garden and hope to protect yourself from trespassers. But they'll come anyway. Then you'll have to grow thicker hedges with sharper thorns. As the water of forgiveness floods over us, it softens us and what we grow. Soaked in forgiveness, flowers bloom over the thorns. Lord, let me grow gentle words rather than thorny hedges.

This water of forgiveness is an especially dark cover. While the blood of Jesus cleanses us, forgiveness is also the blackest, deepest darkness set over our sins as a cover. Forgiveness places our sins into the utter darkness of the three hours of darkness, those last hours of Jesus on the cross. Our sins are buried with Him, and the complete darkness of the tomb swallows them. Our sins are the most stubborn stain imaginable; they resist our repeated attempts to rub and scrub them out of our lives. But God covers them in the silent flood of the utter darkness of Jesus' death and tomb. There, the darkness of our sins has met its match, a covering of utter darkness, the death of God's Son.

Where Did It Go?—There It Is!

If forgiveness puts our sins in the darkness of the tomb, covering them in the utter dark, we can see only that covering, the death of God's Son. That's a wonderful image of forgiveness for the visual assurance it gives us. But what if we want forgiveness to remove our sins completely with no hope of return?

A flood is good for that. After a flood, you wander around the yard, looking for what was there yesterday. Where did the kids' plastic toys go? Who knows? They're gone with the flood and they're not coming back. So also forgiveness takes sins on the ultimate journey, beyond our sight, with no chance of return. Psalm 103:12 explains this comforting distance: "As far as the east is from the west, so far does He remove our transgressions from us." Our sins? Gone, utterly gone, to the other side of the world.

Perhaps the image of the scapegoat represents this distance best. Leviticus 16:21–22 describes the guilt laid on the goat and its sending:

> And Aaron shall lay both his hands on the head of the live goat, and confess over it all the iniquities of the people of Israel, and all their transgressions, all their sins. And he shall put them on the head of the goat and send it away into the wilderness by the hand of a man who is in readiness. The goat shall bear all their iniquities on itself to a remote area, and he shall let the goat go free in the wilderness.

The goat takes the entire load and carries it out of sight. What an image of innocence bearing the wrongs of others! The goat has done nothing but carries all. What a picture of the innocent Lamb who willingly takes the sins of the world.

But what happens to the goat? Our worst nightmare would be the goat returning to camp, bringing our sins back again. But drive the goat into the wilderness and don't worry. It won't live. It won't return. The goat will die and our sins will die with it. Isn't that a comforting image of the distance and finality of God's placement of our sins on the innocent Lamb? Not only does He carry them outside the camp to Mount Calvary, but He will never bring them back. He was purposely sent to die under the burden. The flood tide of forgiveness runs out to the cross, carrying our sins up that hill. But good news—the sins carried away in that flood never ebb their way back down to us.

On a flood day, you do hope certain things stay in place. While you could probably care less about a couple scraps of paper floating around in the basement, I'm sure you want the foundation to remain where it is, lest the furnace start to move. So it is also with our sins. While we're glad that they have floated out of sight, we also want to know that they are now fixed in place, out of sight. If this flood of forgiveness lasts, where are those sins finally set?

For this need, we have another image of forgiveness. It is the unique active depiction of Jesus' work on the cross. Colossians 2:13–14 shows Jesus' action this way: "And you, who were dead in your trespasses and the uncircumcision of your flesh, God made alive together with Him, having forgiven us all our trespasses, by canceling the record of debt that stood against us with its legal demands. This He set aside, nailing it to the cross." What a powerful moment when we see Jesus not merely as the passive sacrifice, but also as the Carpenter. His calloused hands take up the hammer and nails as He nails not Himself but the decrees that stood against us. His nails go deeply into the cross so that the nails and the charges against us will never come loose. Never will they float upward and come back to accuse us. The cross is not a dangerous driftwood, ready to come ashore against us. It is the wood of forgiveness that silences the charges against us. The blows of His hammer speak for us so that there is no one left to accuse or condemn us (Romans 8:33–34). We are forgiven both by the depth and distance of His forgiveness and by the silencing of the charges against us.

His calloused hands take up the hammer and nails as He nails not Himself but the decrees that stood against us.

Can You Spare Some Water?

When forgiveness cleanses and covers us, when it both takes our sins out of sight and nails them to the cross, then we're ready to face our neighbor. Remember the opening picture in this chapter about the neighbor who comes asking for some of the floodwater pumping out of my basement? He notices that I seem to have quite a bit of water around my place and he would like some if I can spare it.

Imagine the insanity if I were to say, "No! Go get your own. I'm keeping this water for myself." Sure, I might have water pushing through every pore of my foundation, but I'm hoarding it, creating a moat with the excess water to keep my neighbor away from me.

Is there any less insanity in our refusal to forgive our neighbor? He notices that we seem to be awash in forgiveness, and he would like to have a bit. He doesn't want to drain us dry but he would like to have just enough to cover some corner of his life. Yet, even though we're swamped, we try to gather this forgiveness up and seize it for ourselves. The problem is the same as trying to clutch a handful of water. If you hoard water and want to grasp it in clenched hands, how much water do you get? The harder you hold it, the less you have. The more you protect it from others, the less that is left for you. We lose this forgiveness when we squeeze it for ourselves alone. When we've fended off everyone who might have some from us, we find that forgiveness has slipped past our grasp.

Forgiveness is water poured from heaven that covers over us and runs freely beyond us. Like water, forgiveness fills everything up to a certain height. If it has come up as high as you and has covered your sins, it must cover everyone we might consider lower than ourselves. If we're forgiven, then the level of forgiveness covers those around us also. If we can't imagine forgiveness reaching our neighbors, who we consider to be beneath us, then it certainly will never reach us.

But we forgive because forgiveness has reached us and others on the equal floodplain. This helps us understand the difficult conjunction in the Lord's Prayer that joins the two halves of the Fifth Petition, "Forgive us our trespasses *as* we forgive those who trespass against us" (emphasis added). In Matthew 6:12, the conjunction is a relatively simple "as." In Greek, ὡς, *hos*, is a relative adverb serving as a conjunction, with possible meanings of "as, so, because." In Luke 11:4, the conjunction is a pair of words, καὶ γάρ, *kai gar*, and has the meaning "for also, for even." The conjunctions themselves may grammatically allow for either an action that precedes God's forgiveness or one that follows His forgiveness. However, the question is not the temporal sequence but rather the relationship between God's forgiveness and our forgiving others. By praying, we don't change the mind of an unmerciful God. Rather, we ourselves are changed to show mercy. We ask that God would forgive us so that we might have the forgiveness

> The cross is not a dangerous driftwood, ready to come ashore against us. It is the wood of forgiveness that silences the charges against us.

we need to forgive others. Where would we get forgiveness for our neighbor if we were not first overwhelmed ourselves? If God were forgiving us on an eye-for-an-eye basis, whereby He says, "I'll forgive you as much as I see you forgive others," then we'd have no reason to be different from our neighbor. "I'll forgive him when I see him forgive me" becomes an enormous game of dominoes with the whole world waiting for someone to give way first. If no one will fall first and forgive a neighbor, then everyone, from man to God, will stay standing in their pride and say, "Well, you can't expect me to forgive until you do."

And so, God fell first. "He was despised and rejected by men, a man of sorrows and acquainted with grief; . . . He was pierced for our transgressions; He was crushed for our iniquities; . . . and the LORD has laid on Him the iniquity of us all" (Isaiah 53:3, 5, 6). God, the standing judge, becomes the fallen criminal. The One who should condemn us dies, rises, and intercedes on our behalf (Romans 8:34). We pray because He first prays for us. His intercession is the sound of forgiveness raining down on us. If you ever woke up to the sound of rain and were glad of it, imagine that sound now as the echo of the Son's words to the Father for us. Rain on the roof is heaven's rhythm section and is the Morse code of the Son speaking for us.

Proof When We Need It

Return a final time to the request of my neighbor for some of the water that's flooding my basement. I'm glad he asks for it—so glad, in fact, that I help him set up a pump and lay out his own hose. Soon there's a steady stream of water from my basement to his place. Now imagine the next day. After you've gone to bed and dreamed that a flood has surrounded your house and filled your basement, you wake with a start and shake your head. Could that really have happened? Still half asleep, you look around and notice everything looks normal: the house is still standing and the whole first floor is as dry as a five-year-old dust bunny. But then you see a hose going from your basement straight to your neighbor's yard. It wasn't a dream or nightmare. The flood really happened. Your neighbor proves it.

Forgiving your neighbor does the same for you today. It reassures you that the dream of being forgiven actually happened. Your neighbor is right here. If he is forgiven, then it's through the forgiveness of God seeping into you and through you to him. Luther called the forgiven neighbor a Means of Grace and a great comfort:

> Thus we are abundantly taken care of, and we can
> find grace and mercy everywhere. Where would you

look for it any closer than with your neighbor, with whom you live every day and toward whom every day you have ample reason to practice this forgiveness? . . . It is, therefore, not only in the church or in the presence of the priest, but in the very midst of our own life, that we have a daily sacrament or baptism, one brother with another and everyone at home in his house. For if you take hold of the promise through this work, you have the very thing that you receive in Baptism. How could God have endowed us more richly with His grace than by hanging such a common baptism around our necks and attaching it to the Lord's Prayer, a baptism that everyone discovers in himself when he prays and forgives his neighbor?[20]

The forgiveness of God comes as near at hand as our families and neighbors. The gifts of heaven, as Luther says, come to hang around our necks. We couldn't ask for a closer proof of forgiveness. Therefore, we forgive because God has forgiven first, and we follow Him as a celebration and reassurance of our own forgiveness.

Living after the Flood

The day after the 1997 flood was a Sunday. It was sunny and warm, which allowed us to spread our soaked belongings from the basement on the lawn in hopes of drying them out. It was surprising to see how much of what we had hidden in the basement was brought out for anyone to see. As we worked, neighbors asked if we needed help. Later we went over to our neighbors' house to lift out a soaked carpet. Since we had been in their shoes the day before, it was distinctly familiar, even though we had never been in their basement before the flood. There was a new openness between the neighbors because we had all gone through the same experience.

The Fifth Petition has the same effect for us today. The flood of forgiveness has settled over us. Because it's swept over each of us, there is a change in our relationships. We ask for the Father to do what He's already pressing on us. Of course He will forgive. He already has. Listen to the water of forgiveness lapping against you already. Our neighbor

20   LW 21:151.

has opened his doors and asked us to send some of this forgiveness his way. When we see it spreading over him, then we know this is more than a dream. It is the central hope and reality of the prayer, the covering flood; we are forgiven.

.

CHAPTER SIX

{ Catch Me! }

I ONCE WENT TO A WATER PARK WHERE PARENTS WERE ENCOURAG-
ING THEIR CHILDREN TO WADE INTO THE WAVE POOL. At the time,
the wave machine was shut off and the water was calm. I watched as
several children cautiously walked into the water and climbed onto
inner tubes. Imagine the children overcoming their fears of water
and waves, beginning to enjoy the pool. They paddle out toward their
parents on their brightly colored tubes and, perhaps, think, "This isn't
so bad." But then the horn sounds. They don't know this means the
wave machine is about to start. The pool begins heaving with two- and
three-foot waves. This isn't a wading pool anymore, and their inflat-
ables aren't going to last.

In the Sixth Petition of the Lord's Prayer, the water surrounding
us has reached new depths. The showers of daily bread have come in
their time. Then the deluge of forgiveness has swept over us, carrying
us beyond our own borders to our neighbors. These gifts are a benevolent tide that lifts us up so our feet are barely touching the ground. Like
riding a wave, we're carried with a buoyancy that suspends us between
earth and heaven.

But waves can carry us too far if we're not careful. We can be swept
out to sea, lose touch with the ground and sky, and be submerged. But
before this happens, we might think we're invincible, like children
sailing away with the waves on bright, inflatable inner tubes. We can
lose sight of the bottom, and even the shore becomes hazy.

More than in the calm moments, we need a father right then.
We need a dad to come when our raft overturns in a wave much larger
than we expected. It's when we're tumbling in the surf, when we're
in the center of a kaleidoscope of sky, water, and beach that we need
a strong hand to catch us. We need a dad who somehow stands only

knee-deep in this churning surf. He plucks us up and says, "That's far enough." We need a Father who somehow can say to the storm and wind, "Quiet down."

We pray in the Sixth Petition for our Father to catch us. We're tempted to blindly paddle out farther than we should. Whether He catches us before we set out, snatches us as the raft is about to tip, or pulls us up when we've already taken in three full gulps of water, the hope is the same: "Catch me!" We pray that the Father would help us to use the great wave of gifts He's given us. We don't want to be afraid of His world or its blessings. But we also pray that He would warn us so that we are not blind to the dangers that are there. As adventurous, thankful children, we're setting sail into the world with this call to our Father, "If I go too far, if the sea is too rough, if there's something out there too big for me, catch me!" And so we pray the Sixth Petition: "And lead us not into temptation."

HEAVEN   HEAVEN

OUR FATHER —NAME   KINGDOM & POWER

KINGDOM COME   DELIVER US

WILL BE DONE   LEAD US NOT

DAILY BREAD   FORGIVENESS

EARTH

One of the significant changes that this petition brings is a return to the Father's hand as the central request. In the Second and Third Petitions, asking for His kingdom and His will to come, we said to the Father, "You come too." We took His hand and urged Him to come with us. In the petitions for bread and forgiveness, we have Him with us and are asking for His two great gifts that sustain us on earth. We haven't forgotten Him in the midst of these gifts, but we focus on His gifts in these petitions. Now in the Sixth Petition, we're awash in His gifts that fill our world. We're not asking for one particular thing. We're once again children looking for our Father's hand. The key difference between the first request for His hand in His kingdom and will and our prayer now is that of direction. In the Second and Third Petitions, we are leaving the heavenly chorus

> *God is already both steering us away from temptation and putting a leash on temptation to drag it farther from us, so we're not overwhelmed.*

of praise and returning to earth's concerns. At the prayer's start, we're taking our Father with us as we take up our daily work. Now in the Sixth Petition, we're turning our attention away from the earth and asking the Father to take us home again to heaven. The gifts of food and forgiveness are wonderful, but they're not enough to keep us here. We know there's danger around us and that heaven is waiting for us. "Father, take us to You." In the beginning of the prayer, we asked God to join us as we returned to our chores—"You come too," we prayed. Now, as children awash in a flood, we need our Father to snatch us up and say, "You come home."

While the Sixth Petition seems to focus on the dark water of temptation, which is far too deep for us, it actually is a wonderfully secure petition. We ask the Father to keep us from the tempter's overwhelming power and our own blindness. There is nothing uncertain about the intention of the Father for our good. Since this petition comes after the Father has fed and forgiven us, He is certainly going to preserve us. As with forgiveness, we can pray this petition with the certainty of 1 John 5:14–15, knowing that we are asking for what God wishes us to have and therefore we have it. We're like children climbing up a playground ladder, calling to our father who's standing behind us, "Watch me. But catch me if I fall." When we ask Him to catch us, He says, "I already have."

Do We Even Need to Ask This?

The certainty of the Sixth Petition leads us to a reasonable question: "Do we even need to ask a gracious Father and an unerring God to lead us not into temptation? Doesn't He by nature always oppose temptation?" If this petition is necessary, a simple reading of it would wrongly suggest that God leads us into temptation. In that view, we're overwhelmed children asking our Father to take some of His own burden off our shoulders. Or even more frightening, it may for some suggest that God is only barely in charge of our lives and that the tempter has a greater power over us. If that's the case, then we're asking God to do what little He can to keep us from being overwhelmed. Yet, each of these understandings clearly undercuts the goodness and power of God.

> When we ask Him to catch us, He says, "I already have."

One perspective that helps with this question is a return to the principle that guided the first three petitions. In asking for God's name to be hallowed and His kingdom and will to come, we're asking for things God has already established, is doing, and will bring about fully in His own time. We're asking that God would do these things among us also and in such a way that we're more conscious and active in them. In asking God to lead us not into temptation, we have the same principle at work. God is already not leading us into temptation, that is, a temptation of an uncontrolled sort. God is already both steering us away from temptation and putting a leash on temptation to drag it farther from us, so we're not overwhelmed. So when we pray, "Lead us not into temptation," the focus is on our weakness to temptation while God's power over evil is preserved. James 1:13–14 is clear: "Let no one say when he is tempted, 'I am being tempted by God,' for God cannot be tempted with evil, and He Himself tempts no one. But each person is tempted when he is lured and enticed by his own desire." We might say this petition with the certainty we have concerning His name, kingdom, and will: "Your name is holy, Your kingdom and will are coming, and You do not lead Your children into temptation. Do these things among us also so that we trust Your work all the more."

Never in the Worst Time or Place

For many years now, I've enjoyed driving old cars, trucks, and motorcycles, often for many miles at a time. Over the years, we've had a 1930 Model A Ford sedan and still have a 1917 Model T Ford touring car. There was a Ducati motorcycle given to us for free, and I once purchased a Ford truck for only $400. None of these vehicles were ever in perfect shape. Driven for work, they were out in the rain, snow, or dark. There have been burnt wires, burst hoses, leaking pumps, flat tires, fouled plugs, and more. But there's been one constant in all these problems: the trouble that came was never the worst that could come, and it never came in the worst time or place.

On February 18, some years ago, I left our home at 5:00 a.m. to drive our 1930 Ford Model A sedan to Wausau, Wisconsin, about 115 miles away, in order to speak that morning at a conference. At 7:00 a.m., I was driving across a bridge when I happened to hear a small tink. I glanced in the rearview mirror just in time to see something bouncing across the road behind me. I pulled over and checked under the hood. The generator pulley had split in two. This left me with no generator to charge the battery or run the lights and no water pump or fan to cool the engine. I walked back over the bridge and found the broken pieces of the pulley. Since I was still 35 miles from Wausau, I drove slowly into town, thankful that it was about thirty degrees that morning. Steam boiled out of the radiator, but it was cold enough outside that I was able to make those last miles without hurting the engine.

The problem would be coming home. The car couldn't go 115 miles without a water pump or a generator. I was nervous about this when I pulled into the meeting. I spoke to the group on my appointed topic, though in the back of my mind I was wondering how I would ever get home. I told only one person about the problem. During a break, he shared my story with a woman who, unbeknown to him, worked as the secretary for the Ford dealer in Wausau. She called the service department, told them to take me in, and after my talk, led me and the Model A to the shop. They welded the pulley together for me. I installed it, topped off the radiator, and drove home.

That day could have been so different if the worst had happened at the worst time. What if the pulley had broken in the dark and I hadn't heard the tink and seen the part tumble across the road, or if the bridge hadn't stopped the broken pulley's roll, or if I had been driving on a hot day? But it all worked out in the end and it was one of the most memorable, if not exactly enjoyable, drives of my life.

In the Lord's Prayer, we're asking for God to put a limit on the worst that the tempter would do to us. We ask that God would put a muzzle on this beast that would devour us and that, when trouble comes, the trouble would be under His control. Our prayer knows that God has power over Satan and that nothing happens outside of His own control. There is a central mystery to this prayer whereby God, who opposes Satan and evil and does not wish His children to fall, still allows temptation and harnesses it for His own purpose. To our reason, this is an impossible contradiction. Our expectation is that God would simply crush Satan and all temptation. Instead, He allows it to come, though He is not the beginning of our temptation. He does, however, limit the nature of it.

Pray even when IT IS TOO LATE.

The boys died. It wasn't expected; two boys died suddenly, one during Elijah's ministry and one during Elisha's. Too late for prayer? Yes, but . . . both Elijah and Elisha immediately prayed, and continued to pray, "Let this child's life come into him again." And the boys lived (1 Kings 17:17–24; 2 Kings 4:18–37)! When the sweep of danger has overtaken you and the worst has come, pray even then. Pray for the consoling, powerful hand of God who has plans larger than ours. The dead might not rise, but the living Lord always hears, and who knows what miracles He has planned, even when it seems too late.

This is a difficult balance to see. The Formula of Concord, Solid Declaration, Article XI describes well God's oversight of evil, His control of it, and His final turning of it:

Foreknowledge or prevision means that God sees and

knows everything before it happens. This is called God's foreknowledge, which extends over all creatures, good and bad. In other words, He foresees and foreknows everything that is or will be, that is happening or will happen, whether it is good or bad. . . . God's foreknowledge foresees and foreknows what is evil, yet not in the sense that it is God's gracious will that evil should happen. Everything that the perverse, wicked will of the devil and of people wants and desires to try and do, God sees and knows before it happens. His foreknowledge preserves order also in wicked acts or works, since a limit and measure is fixed by God for the evil that God does not will. He limits how far it should go, how long it should last, and when and how He will hinder and punish it. (paragraphs 4, 6)

God's oversight of evil has no part in creating evil, but His powerful hand still directs the evil that surrounds us. He not only limits it but even turns it to the benefit of His people. The Confessions use Psalm 103:19 for this point: "The Lord has established His throne in the heavens, and His kingdom rules over all."

Remember your own temptations. No matter how powerful they appear, temptations cannot demand that we follow them. They never come with the worst force or timing which would compel us to follow them. Though we continue to dwell in our bodies of sin and death, we're not demanded at this moment to follow this particular temptation that we're facing. Our new life in Christ has already assured us that we won't be tempted in such a way that there's no escape. In this petition, we're praying that God would shelter us from temptations so that some never reach us and we can look for the escape He's provided for the temptations that remain.

Temptations come, but God can also limit the time and manner in which they appear. When they arrive, we're also reminded that our temptations are not unusual; they are the same temptations that Christians have struggled with throughout the centuries. The problems I've had with my Model A water pump leaking or Model T tires going flat are all great conversation pieces with older men. Each one of them has a story about the same thing happening to them. In fact, most of them can tell a much better story, something like two tires going flat at once while going downhill with no brakes. When I wonder what I've done wrong to my old Ford to deserve these problems, they just laugh and say, "They all did that." Paul reminds us of this principle in 1 Corinthians 10:13: "No temptation has overtaken you that is not common to man." Before you complain to God that the hardest and strongest temptations have come to you, and you're tempted to shake your fist, saying, "It's not fair! What did I do to deserve this?" feel a calming hand on your shoulder and hear God say, "They're all like that. Everyone faces temptations. I'm not unfair, and I haven't turned My back on you." It doesn't take away the trial, but it reminds us of all those who are in it with us.

Another thing about these problems being common is that they all have a fix. In the summer of 1988, I bought my Model T for $250. Before then, it had sat outside in the elements for thirty-five years on a northern Wisconsin farm. It was a rotting hulk. After I rebuilt the engine, I was ready to start it for the first time on Father's Day. I had never started a T before. But my father, a former army mechanic, was there, and his first car had been a Model T. Also in our garage that day was our neighbor Louie, who, with his brothers, was a Ford dealer and owner of several Model Ts. We also had Lynn, a friend who had much experience with old Fords. That Sunday wasn't work for them; it was a day they traveled back in time. Turn that crank, buzz those coils, and adjust that carb. That afternoon, they were all young men again. Every problem had an answer. For instance, when the engine started, the water pump leaked. Lynn said, "Wait here." He went home and brought back an old box of vintage water pump packing string. We put the packing in that day, it's worked every

"Lord, lead us into temptation no greater than theirs. Lead us to an end no less than theirs."

day since, and I still have the box. Every problem had a solution. I just had to ask the men who knew.

The Sixth Petition is our way of asking for the solutions. Our problems are not unheard of, certainly not to our Father. There's a solution, and the asking for it is in the prayer. "Lead us not into temptation" asks that we would see the answer to the temptations we face.

The continuing part of the verse quoted earlier from 1 Corinthians 10:13 is, "God is faithful, and He will not let you be tempted beyond your ability, but with the temptation He will also provide the way of escape, that you may be able to endure it." We can rest secure in the knowledge that our Father sees the answer for our temptation before the temptation even comes.

Imagine the great, encircling crowd we joined in the Lord's Prayer when we said, "Our Father who art in heaven." In this company of saints, we have those who have faced every trial that we have today, and much more. In my garage that Father's Day, I had more than a hundred years of mechanics' experiences with old Fords. But imagine what we have when we pray, "Lead us not into temptation." When we bring our needs to God and cringe before the oncoming trial, the saints of over four thousand years can sympathetically say, "I understand," and then go on to tell a far more dramatic story than our own. They have seen the proof that God limits temptation and provides an escape. They're the heroes of the faith and the great cloud of witnesses that surrounds us (Hebrews 12:1). They urge us to finish the race ahead of us. They would never say of our temptations, "That's a new one. Not sure how that's going to turn out." Our temptations are no different than theirs. Our prayer is that their experience will be for us a path to follow, a strengthening to face our own temptations. They were tested as we are, yet they are in the cloud of witnesses, the hosts with the Father in heaven. With these saints in mind, our prayer is simple: "Lord, lead us into temptation no greater than theirs. Lead us to an end no less than theirs."

When my Model T wouldn't run at first, I wasn't terribly worried because the other men around me weren't concerned. They'd seen this sort of problem before. But what if we could have had Henry Ford himself in the garage that day? Ford was noted to be a remarkable mechanic himself, and who would know the car better than the one who designed it? I'm sure we would've listened to his advice and done whatever he suggested. After all, what's our experience compared to his?

GROW WISELY WHAT YOU HAVE

"Buy truth, and do not sell it; buy wisdom, instruction, and understanding" (Proverbs 23:23). It's easy to buy seeds and fertilizer, soil and flowers. But good advice is priceless and hard to find. Protect the truth you already know, and weed out the deceptions that pose as flowers but are only noxious weeds. Seek truth and ask to know when you have found it. Lord, teach me to grow wisdom and understanding in the garden of my life.

So we stand in a great company of witnesses, but they might well stand in silence when comparing their temptations and overcoming trials to His. Because what is their experience compared to the Son's? Hebrews 4:15–16 reminds us that no one knows our experience better than He: "For we do not have a high priest who is unable to sympathize with our weaknesses, but one who in every respect has been tempted as we are, yet without sin. Let us then with confidence draw near to the throne of grace, that we may receive mercy and find grace to help in time of need." When temptation bewilders us, Jesus comes near. "For because He Himself has suffered when tempted, He is able to help those who are being tempted" (Hebrews 2:18). He can assure us that as difficult as our temptations are, they are not the worst that can be. For Jesus has seen to that already. "Lead us not into temptation" is buffered with the truth that the worst temptation has passed by us and gone straight to Him. The solution of our temptation has already been found when He overcame it in the desert and on the cross and when He rose from the dead. When we call out, "Father, catch us before we fall," we know that He will catch us, just as on the cross He caught His Son falling into His arms.

Why Have Temptation at All?

If temptation is so costly, why have it at all? If it costs the life of the Son and plagues us still, why not remove it all together? If we had written the Lord's Prayer ourselves, we might rather have asked God to banish all temptation. Don't just lead us away from the tempter. Instead, lead the tempter straight to the fire he deserves. Rather than fencing in millions of sheep, destroy the wolf. This makes the most sense. Why would God allow temptation at all?

This question is much like the cry for daily bread when the

drought has struck our lives. Why would a loving Father let the stones stay dusty when His children need bread? Yet, the greater wonder in that petition is not that we've gone hungry, but that He also was hungry, thirsty, and finally dying. In the same way, we pray, "Lead us not into temptation." We have a deeper mystery besides our own temptation. We remember His own.

Remember what you got for bringing home good grades? Perhaps for every A on your report card, you received money or your favorite meal or a trip to the mall. Now think back to high school. What would you think if your father, after seeing your perfect 4.00 report card, said to you, "I'm very proud of you! Now go to your room, close the door, don't answer the phone, no dinner for you tonight, and stay there until I tell you to come out."

Can you imagine a father saying this to a child who's done everything right? But our Father, after acclaiming Jesus as His Son in Jesus' Baptism (Matthew 3:17), leads His Son into the desert without food for forty days to be tempted. After Jesus' thirty years of perfect life, God seems to close off His Son, leaving Him hungry and tempted. The theme of Jesus' Sonship is a central part of the temptation in those forty days. "If You are the Son of God, command these stones to become loaves of bread. . . . Throw Yourself down [from the temple]" (Matthew 4:3, 6). In these temptations is the challenge to His Sonship: "If You are the Son of God, then certainly He wouldn't want You to suffer. Stop being hungry, stop walking when You can fly, stop looking like less than the Son."

Yet, Jesus accepted the hunger, the demands of gravity, and the temptations that came to Him. This temptation didn't contradict His Sonship but rather confirmed it. Because He was the Son, He was tempted. It wasn't punishment by the Father. It was a demonstration of Sonship to be so tested. Our wonder at being tempted has to start with awe over the temptation of God's Son. If temptation is difficult and testing is severe, who would ever choose to undergo it? We pray to avoid it; He willingly takes it on. Here is a mystery greater than the ultimate origin of evil. God allows temptation upon His perfect Son and does it for our sake. Hebrews 12:2–3 urges us to look "to Jesus, the founder and perfecter of our faith, who for the joy that was set before Him endured the cross, despising the shame, and is seated at the right hand of the throne of God. Consider Him who endured from sinners such hostility against Himself, so that you may not grow weary or fainthearted."

The challenge of this petition is waking to the temptations that come to the children of God. Like children on the ocean's edge, we have to leave a secure beach. It is time to cautiously sail out while still being watchful of the depth that surrounds us. While there is security in a Father who hates the tempter and who has already throttled him, there is still a deep current running around and beneath us. The wonder of the voyage is that we follow the wake of God's Son who willingly sailed before us and went to a greater depth than we will ever face.

Temptations in Our Sleep

For many years I went to the outdoor national motocross race in Buchanan, Michigan, with our son, Steve. This is one of twelve motorcycle races held across the country each summer with the best motocross racers from America and around the world. Honda, Yamaha, Suzuki, Kawasaki, KTM, the biggest names in off-road motorcycling, each send their factory-tuned bikes, enormous trucks, and multimillion dollar teams to race. The racing is incredibly fast over a twisting track set in the Michigan hillside. A crowd of more than twenty-three thousand people comes to stand as close as twenty feet from the track, have dirt sprayed in their faces, and feel the ground shake.

However, seated immediately behind us, just twenty-five feet from the track, during the most important race of the day, a man was sleeping. He was in a lawn chair, his head back, sound asleep. The world's finest motocross racers were leaping into a fifty-foot jump directly in front of him, and he slept. At full throttle, forty racing engines screamed past him, and he slept. The national sports camera crew was filming straight across the track from him, there was a live website broadcast going on, the trackside announcer shot out words like an auctioneer, and he slept. Thousands of people drove hours to see this race, paid twenty-five dollars each to push against the fences, and he slept. He was in racing heaven, and he slept.

I wonder if we don't appear the same to the angels in heaven. We're surrounded by blessings which are, I suspect, far clearer to them than they are to us, yet we seem to sleep through many of them. We have the blessings we've already mentioned throughout the prayer, especially the last two petitions. We have food for every day and a flood of forgiveness, yet we sleep. We say those petitions with a sleepy yawn and a bored, "But of course You're going to feed us and forgive us. You always have. It's somehow in the contract." We hallow His holy name and ask for a place in the choir to praise it. But we might be yawning before we've even finished the first verse. We hurry His kingdom so that He would remember us in it. We hope that His will would be done and that He would walk with us through it. But when we finish all this, our great temptation is simply to sleep.

By the time we get to the Sixth Petition, we might have said the prayer with a yawn. It's all a comfortable cadence. But it's time to wake up! We're children drifting on the Atlantic Ocean on a brightly colored inflatable raft. The mysteries of an unseen world are beneath us. The waves are building with foam around us. The distant shore is disappearing behind us, becoming a fuzzy landscape that we can barely see, and we've closed our eyes to all of this. We've pulled down our caps, settled our shoulders into the raft, and slept.

To the sleeping disciples, who had just finished the inaugural Lord's Supper, Jesus said, "Why are you sleeping? Rise and pray that you may not enter into temptation" (Luke 22:46). They had just heard the words of the last meal of Jesus and experienced what generations of Christians have yearned to share, and yet they slept. They were warned that their three-year drama was coming to a conclusion that very night, but they slept. Their own fall was predicted, but they confidently slept. "Pray so that you will not fall into temptation" was a call to them that they might wake to the coming temptation and also pray that it would be limited to one they could overcome.

God is saying the same to us when we pray the Sixth Petition. We're praying that we might wake up to see the temptation that's around us. The prayer itself might bring to mind some of this temptation. Think of the temptations suggested by the petitions we've just finished. Jesus puts the Sixth Petition here in the prayer so that we might think of temptations possible in each of the steps we have already traveled and in those that are coming. Somewhat like the Fifth Petition, it is one of the central steps of the journey.

In this central place, forgiveness and temptation are a natural

Forgive us in a washing flood, but don't let us forget the costly price of every drop. Forgive us, but catch us before we're swept away.

pair. In the midst of these blessings from God, we need a Father who rules with a firm hand. Send us to forgive others, but don't send us too far from You. Send us into lives desperately distant from You, but don't let us out of Your grasp. Forgive us so richly that we never doubt, but never let us imagine that this forgiveness was easy or automatic. Forgive us in a washing flood, but don't let us forget the costly price of every drop. Forgive us, but catch us before we're swept away.

As we just noted, this theme of temptation is a central idea of the Lord's Prayer. It connects with more than the Fifth Petition of forgiveness. Think of the steps of each petition in light of temptation. When we arrive at the Sixth Petition, we look back, realizing the temptations possible in each step we've already traveled and those to come.

> In the First Petition, we pray that we might not dishonor His name, stand silent in the chorus that is praising Him, or sing in life so off-key that men hear more of us than Him.

> In the Second Petition, we pray that we won't deny the coming of His kingdom, be found sleeping when the Bridegroom arrives, or so doubt His grace that we hide from His coming.

> In the Third Petition, we pray that we will be those in whom He works to desire and accomplish His good pleasure so that we are not ungratefully independent in this life and abandoned by Him in the next.

> Next, in the Fourth Petition, we pray that as we wait for His daily bread we won't doubt its soon coming, despite our drought, and when it comes, we pray that we'll remember who sent the day's shower.

> In the Fifth Petition, we pray that we will be so flooded with forgiveness that we cannot help but be soaked through and overflow to our neighbors.

> Here in the Sixth Petition, we pray that we will be awake to overcome the temptations that swirl around us, hissing like the ocean's foam, promising safety but capturing us in their undertow.

> In the final petition, we pray that we will recognize the evil one who would capture us and that we

will welcome our Father's firm grip upon us.

As we conclude our prayer, we pray that we'll
be found singing always in the final steps
toward His kingdom, power, and glory.

The gifts of the Lord's Prayer are somewhat like the Garden of Eden itself. It was created in holiness and yet was the starting place for our temptation. The perfect world became the setting for all the world's trials. So, the perfect prayer reminds us of the temptations that can come even with the blessings of God's name, presence, bread, and forgiveness. If we could return to Eden and warn Adam and Eve, we would shout to them, "Wake up! Don't you see the serpent coming?" The angels and the saints are likely saying the same to us today. "Watch out, the devil is still slithering about. He wants to cling to all you have just received, the daily bread, the forgiveness, and even the promise of protection." Why Adam and Eve would ever be tempted in the midst of a perfect setting is a mystery. Yet, it was true for them and is still true for every Christian today. As impossible and irrational as it seems, we still at times forsake the Holy Spirit's leading and follow the tempter instead.

In the midst of these blessings from God (His name, presence, daily bread, and forgiveness), we need a Father who puts a firm hand on us and catches us before we're seduced by the serpent. We need a Son who has trapped the serpent's head under His heel. The serpent still bares his fangs, but it's over. Jesus can say, "I died, and behold I am alive forevermore, and I have the keys of Death and Hades" (Revelation 1:18). Let the serpent strike as he will. The Son is immune to him, and we only wait for the final crushing. As we gather round, the Son says, "Stay back. He's still trying to bite." Our prayer is a simple, "Keep him away from me." The Son puts a warning hand out on us, keeping us clear.[21] In the next petition, we ask for Him to finally crush our old enemy.

---

21 Luther has a complementary picture of Satan as a serpent attempting to entice us while prayer restrains him: "'Dear Father, You have asked me to pray. Don't let me fall because of temptations.' Then you will see that the temptations must stop and finally confess themselves conquered. If you try to help yourself by your own thoughts and counsel, you will only make the matter worse and give the devil more space. For he has a serpent's head [Revelation 12:9]. If it finds an opening into which it can slip, the whole body will follow without stopping. But prayer can prevent him and drive him back" (Large Catechism, Part III, paragraphs 110–11).

Taking His Hand

"Lead us not into temptation" puts our hand firmly into the Father's. We ask that He would snatch us out of the tempter's range. Before we begin to complain that there's any temptation at all, we remember the temptations that have already come to the saints before us. We sang in their chorus at the start of the prayer. Now they're nodding with understanding as we face the temptations they once experienced themselves. Then they part company to let us see the One who was tempted in every respect and says, "I know just how it is." In His hand, we know that there is an answer to the temptations we face. With those nail-scarred hands, He'll catch us.

CHAPTER SEVEN

{ It's Time to Go Home Again }

"IT'S TIME TO GO HOME." REMEMBER HEARING THOSE WORDS WHEN YOU WERE A CHILD? You were visiting your aunt and uncle's house. Actually, your parents were visiting. You were waiting. There was no one for you to talk to and nothing to do but notice that the dust was getting really thick on the glass figurines on the third shelf. You put your coat on half an hour ago, and you've been snapping the doorknob back and forth for the last ten minutes. Finally, your mother says, "Well, I suppose it's time to go home." No one has to say it twice for you. You're the first to say, "Good-bye." You take your dad's hand and are surprised that you don't have to drag him along. He got to the car door just as fast as you did. Jump in the car, close the doors, start the engine, let's get moving. It's time to go home.

It's time to go home. Often these words are our escape and relief. "It's time to go home" are the wonderful words you heard at the end of that first frightening day of kindergarten. As you looked up, there was your mom or dad standing at the door with your coat in hand. "It's time to go home" is your dad taking your hand and walking you out of school the day Christmas vacation starts, a glorious two weeks of freedom, Christmas presents, and the food that comes only once a year.

"It's time to come home" is when you reach the end of your experiment with a new job and big city living a thousand miles from home. It wasn't what you'd expected. You tried for six months, maybe a year, all the while wishing time and again that you could go back home. Then one day, you were talking to your dad. You told him all the things that weren't going right, how you'd tried at work and tried to make the apartment feel like home, but nothing seemed to work. He listened, and then the two of you finally said, at the very same moment, "It's time to come home." Thanks be to God, there was a home to go to. Dad was waiting in the driveway when you pulled in, and there was not one "I told you so" in sight. Looking back on those months away from home, you didn't fail. You just found out when it was time to come home.

That's the picture of the Seventh Petition of the Lord's Prayer. Finding when it's time to come home and wanting to go home is our biggest step. We've been away from home, and now it's time to go back. With all the words before about sin, forgiveness, and temptation, it's true that not everything has gone the way we planned. Despite all that, home takes hold of us. Our Father draws us to Himself. He says the words for us, and we're glad to say them with Him, "It's time to come home."

Thanks be to God, there was a home to go to. Dad was waiting in the driveway when you pulled in, and there was not one "I told you so" in sight.

Our homecoming takes time, of course. When you're in Alabama and packing to move back home to Minnesota, it's a long process. But once you've decided to come home, think of the change that comes over you every day. In order to move, you have to go to the bank, the post office, and work. You tell everyone you meet, just for the sound of it, "It's time. I'm going home." You drive all night and fly past every scenic turnoff. If anyone asks why you don't stop, you just say, "I'm going home."

We're on the final steps of our journey home. The Lord's Prayer is practice for finally going home. Every time we pray, we sum up our lives, our creation that echoes heaven, our years of wandering under the clouds, and finally our going home. By the Seventh Petition, we've grown weary of this trip. Perhaps at one point or another we were like children, caught up with the games we have yet to play, or we had just started out in our life and there were jobs and families and homes to build here on earth. But with a little time, we find ourselves saying with our Father, "It's time to come home." We pray, "But deliver us from evil."

Our Father's Hand

When we started the Lord's Prayer, we were caught up by the Father's hand and lifted into the court of heaven. He was there, and so were our words. Then we took His hand and led Him here to earth, where His kingdom and will were still to come. We knew we wouldn't be here long, so we asked if He would come here too. When the way turned tempting and dangerous and the path was about to be flooded over, He caught us with His hand. He had us look up, back to heaven and the home He has made for us. Once more He takes our hand and says, "It's time to come home." If the Seventh Petition has a sensation that you can feel, it's the firm lifting of the Father's hand, drawing you up, and you finding yourself saying with the Father at the same moment the same words, "It's time to come home."

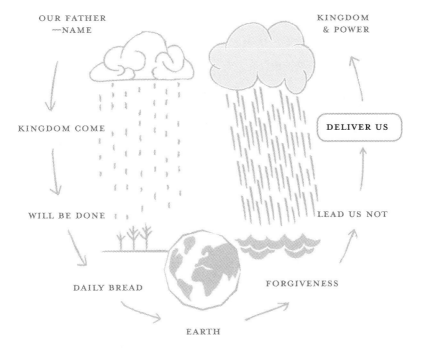

HEAVEN   HEAVEN

OUR FATHER   KINGDOM
—NAME   & POWER

KINGDOM COME   DELIVER US

WILL BE DONE   LEAD US NOT

DAILY BREAD   FORGIVENESS

EARTH

We're a bit older by now in the prayer. In the Second and Third Petitions, we're children, pulling our Father to come with us. Remember the impatience of our tugging on Him? There's a world waiting, and we want Him to come with us. We want to see what the Father can do in His kingdom and will. We're impatient. Nothing on earth is exactly like it should be, so come with us, Father, and make it different. We're going from heaven to earth, and the downhill slope is carrying us fast. There's work to be done, and we don't want to do it alone. You come too.

But now it's time to come home. We've waited out droughts and have been flooded with forgiveness. Temptations have come and we're ready to have our Father take us home. The tugging in this petition is all from the Father. He's cleared a way for us to come home and has promised that our room is ready.

Remember the flood that surrounded our house and filled our basement? I told you that our neighbor's daughters sailed around the neighborhood on a pink air mattress. Now imagine trouble. What if there had been a fully functioning storm drain, four feet in diameter, under that floodwater? Normally that drain has a grid over it to protect five-year-old sailors. But imagine that the drain cover is gone. Do five-year-olds know this? Do they know where their pink air mattress is headed? Not a chance. What they need is a father who sees the danger, wades into the flood, and snatches them up just before they are taken under. He says, "You come home." That's our Father, who sees the currents around us and takes us firmly home.

Don't imagine that Satan's promises come from a generous heart. He plans to winsomely destroy us.

An Answer for the Evil One

But the journey home is not a simple wading through small ripples. "Deliver us from evil" gives us a final look at our Father's most severe enemy, the serpent. Traditionally, the prayer speaks of "evil," though the Greek text does not demand that the translation be either "evil" or "evil one." It is likely that both the individual, Satan, and his resulting evil can be rightly understood under this petition. A general evil of cancer, broken hearts, and poverty is easily included today as the evil which the prayer means. The greater challenge for some is seeing evil as an individual tempter. Yet, the New Testament clearly knows of Satan as the source of the outward evils we face. Using the same word as found in the Lord's Prayer, Jesus speaks elsewhere of the "evil one," such as in John 17:15, "I do not ask that You take them out of the world, but that You keep them from the evil one." In the explanation of Jesus' parable of the sower (Matthew 13:19), Satan is the "evil one [who] comes and snatches away what has been sown." The "evil one" is used as a synonym for the devil in Matthew 13:38–39, where Jesus explains the parable of the weeds: "The weeds are the sons of the evil one, and the enemy who sowed them is the devil." It is God's conquest of Satan that is most crucial for the prayer.

We must be rescued from the evil one at the source of his power, which is his claim that he is like God. Ever since the Garden of Eden, we've been caught up with this lie that Satan first convinced himself of, and then extended to us. We've heard the temptation to worship him as God so that the world will be at our feet. However, don't imagine that Satan's promises come from a generous heart. He plans to winsomely destroy us. Our prayer is that our Father would show His true divine power in throttling the evil one and declaring Himself the only God.

If God would deliver us from the evil one and his claim to have power over us, then our perspective on evil changes. Then we become people of Romans 8:31–35, 38–39:

> [31]What then shall we say to these things? If God is for us, who can be against us? [32]He who did not spare His own Son but gave Him up for us all, how will He not also with Him graciously give us all things? [33]Who shall bring any charge against God's elect? It is God who justifies. [34]Who is to condemn? Christ Jesus is the one who died—more than that, who was raised—who is at the right hand of God, who indeed is interceding for us. [35]Who shall separate us from the love of Christ? Shall tribulation, or distress, or persecution, or famine, or nakedness, or danger, or sword? . . .

> [38]For I am sure that neither death nor life, nor angels nor

rulers, nor things present nor things to come, nor powers,
³⁹nor height nor depth, nor anything else in all creation,
will be able to separate us from the love of God in Christ
Jesus our Lord.

Look at the astonishing list of evil that Paul withstands in verses 35, 38–39 when he says that nothing will separate him from the love of God in Christ Jesus. He is ready to face a blast of trouble, hardship, persecution, famine, nakedness, danger, and sword (v. 35). In verses 38–39, he welcomes every challenger, even demons and death, angels and heights, present and future, and powers, all which try to separate him from God. He is like a man who goes into his yard, hoping that the storm in the west is coming his way. He welcomes the wind and smiles at the hail. When he hears the freight-train sound of the tornado, he shouts, "Bring it on! I've been waiting!" His face is always toward the wind, and he's sad to see the last lightning bolt fade in the east.

Pray even when
IT'S ONLY TO SEE THE SAME TROUBLE AGAIN.

Paul prayed over and over. He asked three times for the thorn in his flesh to be removed. But the thorn remained. What prayer was left? The prayer to see weakness changed to strength, the thorn turned into a gift. God's mercy makes this change: "For My power is made perfect in weakness." When the trouble's not leaving, pray to see it in a new light, the light of "My grace is sufficient for you" (2 Corinthians 12:7–10).

How does Paul stand under the storm that is coming? And how is one able to believe this deliverance has already come, when trouble, hardship, and danger are still here? How do we believe that we're on our way home with the Father when the evil one seems, at least at times, to hold us firmly here on earth?

A wonderful companion to the Lord's Prayer in answering these worries is in Paul's understanding in Romans 8:31–35, listed above. Notice the step-by-step nature of these verses that Paul highlights by four "who" questions in verses 31, 33, 34, and 35. One way to see this structure is to allow each of the questions to refer to a different person, each one acting in a small legal drama. The overall scene is a courtroom with a plaintiff, a prosecuting attorney, and a judge. Verses 31, 33, and 34 suggest these roles with their questions concerning those who prosecute and the one who can condemn. Paul begins with the first of the questions: "If God is for us, who can be against us?" (v. 31). This throws open the whole world as possible plaintiffs, charging us with our wrongs; there is no lack of possible enemies. Think of those against whom we have trespassed and who have our tracks to prove it. These are the enemies who are against us. While Paul's question, "If God is for us, who can be against us?" can be answered with a silent, "No one," the remainder of Paul's words highlights the many enemies that do come against us. It is not that with God we have no enemies, but that along with our enemies we have God.

But accounting for our enemies in the presence of God is just the beginning. The next step in the drama is verse 33, where Paul asks, "Who shall bring any charge against God's elect?" We move beyond the plaintiff to the general courtroom and find there the prosecuting attorney. Here we might especially see Satan as the prosecutor, recalling Job 1 and 2 and his charges against the faithfulness of Job. If Job's remarkable life is an opportunity for the prosecutor, what a feast our lives must be. When we pray, "Deliver us from evil," we might hope that the answer to our prayer would be that the prosecutor somehow misses us in the back of

It is not that with God we have no enemies, but that along with our enemies we have God.

the courtroom. However, there is little chance of his missing any of us. Our deliverance is more than simply being hidden. Hiding is not the saved life. A more permanent deliverance is needed in the confrontation between the prosecutor and the Judge, the God who justifies (v. 33). And so in verse 33, Paul challenges the prosecutor to come forward. Just as he challenged all plaintiffs to come up, he gives the prosecutor the floor first. Let him say all he wishes against us. Paul knows there is a final ruling that is yet to be declared.

So after the plaintiff and the prosecuting attorney speak, the case comes to the third stop, the Judge. Verse 34 brings the Judge in with the third "who" question: "Who is to condemn?" The perfect candidate for Judge is then introduced: "Christ Jesus is the one who died—more than that, who was raised." Here is a Judge who knows the temptations and the schemes of the prosecutor, but He withstood them perfectly. Here is a faultless Judge who is falsely accused. Here is a Judge who has died, but for no fault of His own. Here is a Judge whose death was on our account. He was counted a criminal because we are criminals. Now He steps forward toward the Judge's bench, having come back from the dead.

What mercy could we expect from such a Judge? Look, He still bears the scars our crimes carved into Him. Now He steps to the seat of judgment over us. Satan, the prosecutor, is no longer relevant; his charges are moot. His words against us have faded to useless repetition. What does he really know of our crimes? It is the Judge who has carried them. Now the attention is all on the Judge.

He speaks. We hardly dare to lift our heads when He calls our names. The remainder of verse 34 sums up what His words reveal about us: "[He] who is at the right hand of God, who indeed is interceding for us." This is the most astonishing turnaround. The Judge has been judged by mere men. Though innocent, He has been condemned. And yet, He now speaks on our behalf. We could never presume that God is going to be our defender, but here He dismisses all charges. Romans 8:1 is the verdict: "There is therefore now no condemnation for those who are in Christ Jesus." The accusations against us are silenced because the Judge has taken the brunt of any charge that could be made against us. This is the wonderful reassurance that when we pray the Lord's Prayer, and especially this petition of deliverance from evil, we are doing nothing more than echoing the words already being spoken by the Son to His Father on our behalf. We enter into an inviting court, where a Father is already nodding yes to our request because He first heard it long ago from His Son.

What a change verse 34 makes when it says that He intercedes for us. Imagine being in the courtroom and knowing you are utterly guilty. Only one witness is called, and He is the one whose death you caused. He comes before the Judge, His own Father, and they both look at you. But the only words from the witness are words of mercy and forgiveness, grace and pardon. Amazed, you look at the Judge and see that He is the victim's Father. Even more surprising, He is agreeing with every word from His Son. You can see His face of kindness and you know He agrees with His Son's words when He declares the verdict, "Not guilty." You will never forget that verdict and the words said by the Son, the words that brought your only hope of pardon and peace.

With these words, "not guilty," it would seem then that the drama is over, and in a sense it is. The climax has been reached with the Judge's verdict. This is the moment in which we pray the Lord's Prayer, just as the Judge announces His decision over us. Our cry for deliverance from evil is answered with His words, "Not guilty." There is only one element of the courtroom that we haven't yet addressed. One final "who" question remains in verse 35: "Who shall separate us from the love of Christ?" In a courtroom drama, at the end, who does the separating if the defendant is found guilty? It is the jailer who separates the defendants from their families and takes them to prison. He tears them from loved ones, jobs, homes, friends, and all they've known. The horrors they'd only heard of about prison would become their lives. Notice in verse 35 the following list of possible jailers, those who would separate us from Christ: tribulation, distress, persecution, famine, nakedness, danger, sword. If we didn't have verse 34 and the promise of "Not guilty," all of these would not only separate us from the favor of God but also announce God's condemnation over us. These would-be jailers of trouble, hardship, and persecution want to engulf us in the baggy, blaze-orange jumpsuit that shouts, "God hates you and has left you to the cruel prosecutor!"

However, the jailer can only tear us away from our lives if the Judge finds us guilty. But we are declared not guilty. With that verdict, we're going home. That has been the story throughout this chapter and the triumphant high point of verse 34. The only One who can condemn does not. In verse 37, we're conquerors because He loves us. Therefore, Paul enlarges the list of possible jailers (vv. 38–39), saying that "neither death nor life, nor angels nor rulers, things present nor things to come, nor powers, nor height nor depth, nor anything else in all creation, will be able to separate us from the love of God in Christ Jesus our Lord." He dares anything to challenge the verdict of the Judge. Nothing will prevent us from going home with Him.

This clash with the jailers is the brewing storm that Paul welcomes. These are the blasts of rain and near-miss lightning bolts that he dares. He understands what the prosecutor wishes these storms to mean: "God has abandoned you. You're not His child, not anymore—and He agrees with me. Now you're as lost as I am." All our troubles say the same thing. They all shout that we are lonely and condemned.

But none of that is true. As we pray the Lord's Prayer, we're standing at the moment of the Judge's sentence. The jailer with his life and death, angels and demons is beside us. He may even have laid his hands on us, tugging on us, distracting us so that we can barely hear the Judge's sentence. The jailer may try whispering his own sentence of guilt and doom. But he cannot tear us away from the Judge. The sentence from the bench is, "No condemnation for those who are in Christ Jesus" (8:1).

When the prayer asks then for deliverance from evil, we might especially remember this courtroom. The evil one wants to accuse, to rage, and even to prove our guilt. But our prayer is that we would never forget the deliverance already declared. Our plea is that the Father would turn us away from ourselves. This petition has not a shred of defense on what we have done but points only to the Judge Himself. Deliver us, as Judge, and let no separating, imprisoning trouble whisper that You have condemned us. We pray that we would be delivered from listening to their voices and instead find our deliverance in the sure words of the Judge, "Not guilty."

GROW A GARDEN OF GOOD WORDS

"To make an apt answer is a joy to a man, and a word in season, how good it is!" (Proverbs 15:23). Your own strawberry, grown in your garden, picked by your hand, eaten right then and there—nothing's better. That berry is work and rest, day and night, sun and rain, all in one little bite. The Word of God is a garden, mature fruits and vegetables just waiting for you to pick them off the vine. Savor the garden of good words. The Holy Spirit's guidance sends you exactly to the row you need today. Lord, direct me to the fruit of Your Word that is just what my soul needs today. Make Your gracious words a honeycomb for me (Proverbs 16:24).

This verdict drives the prosecutor back to his corner and leaves us standing, though perhaps encircled by the jailers. Part of the prayer looks ahead to a time when the prosecutor is fully condemned, imprisoned, and so utterly separated from God that we will perhaps not even remember him in heaven. We'll never hear his charges against us, and we'll never waste a tear for the horrors he's facing. But that day is still coming. For the moment now when we pray, we're still at the instant of the Judge's verdict. Each day a different jailer would like to step forward and take his cue from the prosecutor's charges. But each day, our calling is to hear nothing but the verdict of the Judge. "Deliver us from the evil *Deliver us, as Judge, and let no separating, imprisoning trouble whisper that You have condemned us.* of listening to the prosecutor, of despairing over the nearness of the jailers, and of believing that we are on the verge of being separated from You. Never let us believe that dangers, hardships, or even death mark us as hated by You. Right now troubles still stand beside me, but they will never stand between You and me. Deliver me finally from their presence and power. Put me in Your hand and take me home."

The Father's Hand Is on Us

The courtroom drama has gone far enough. Forcing His way past the eager jailers, here comes our Father. He takes our hand, the very hands that the jailers are trying to handcuff. He tells us, "Don't listen to them. Just hold on to Me." When we pray for deliverance, we're rejoicing in the Father's hand taking ours. It becomes a hand of comfort and a hand of adventure. This is the wonderful combination that the Father's hand brings. It is calming assurance because we're led by someone else. It's excitement because He knows more, has been further, and is better acquainted than we are. He's taking us someplace that only He knows. Without His hand, we're locked in place. With His hand, both heaven and earth become our path.

Luther had this powerful hand of God in mind when he concluded his 1530 collection of sayings in which he found comfort. After recalling many of the promises of God's power, he wrote of the confrontation between God and His enemies:

He will always be the one dwelling in heaven no matter how they rage against Him. But He mocks them to encourage us, so that we may take heart and bravely laugh at their onslaughts. Therefore the only thing necessary for us to do is to believe and to pray most confidently in Christ's name that God will give us strength, since He has erected His kingdom and this is His doing. It is He who without our help, counsel, thought, or effort has brought His kingdom forth and has advanced and preserved it to this day. . . . So let us take comfort in His word and, trusting His promise, call upon Him confidently for deliverance in time of distress and He will help.[22]

When we pray, "Deliver us from evil," the naming of evil doesn't increase the power of the evil one or magnify our fears. As Luther says, God mocks the raging of all evil to emphasize His power over every enemy. When we stand within His power, we can speak of evil as a futile wave that tries to overwhelm a towering rock on the shore. We are safe and secure on the rock that will never move. The raging water only magnifies the immovable nature of the rock. And so we build our house upon the rock of His promises (Matthew 7:24–27). David expresses this confidence in Psalm 27: "When evildoers assail me to eat up my flesh, my adversaries and foes, it is they who stumble and fall . . . He will lift me high upon a rock. And now my head shall be lifted up above my enemies all around me" (vv. 2, 5–6) In the Father's hand, upon the rock of His care, we name our enemies, but we do so as secure children held by our Father.

> In praying "deliver us from evil," we're not asking that all evil would be taken away, for then there would be no cross. It is not a petition of complaint, asking, "Why is this happening to me?" It is finding the Father's hand in the dark and believing that it will be all right.

22 LW 43:177.

A Hand of Comfort

Think of a time when someone's hand on yours made all the difference, though your circumstances had not changed. Just two weeks ago, you met your surgeon for the first time, and now you're trying to remember his name as you're wheeled into surgery. But he comes alongside you, asks how you are feeling, and holds your hand. He looks you in the eyes and seems so calm and unhurried. You like the feel of his hand, firm yet comforting. Just before the anesthesia carries you off, as you fail to count another number backward, you remember the feel of his hand.

Perhaps it was another touch that mattered. It was that first spontaneous moment when your future spouse held your hand, or the handshake your father gave when you returned from serving overseas. It was the hand that took yours just before you answered the phone to hear whether you still had your job, the comforting touch that said, "It doesn't matter if you have the job or not. You'll always have me."

All these touches have one thing in common: they change everything for us, though nothing has changed at all. You still need surgery because the tumor is still growing. You still don't know what to say to each other, even though you're holding hands. You made it through basic training, but the army has you for at least four more years. When you answer that phone, you may be out of work. But in a way we can't explain, the surgery and the silence, the coming years and their questions, they all have changed because of that touch. You've found a contentment in that silence. You don't know where you'll be in six months, but you know you can always come home.

The Lord's Prayer gives us the Father's touch. That touch changes us, though much of our world stays the same. He holds us in such a way that we're delivered from evil, though evil is still pressing in on us. Our petition has an unspoken side. While we pray to be delivered from evil, we also are asking to be delivered to His hand. That hand on us is what makes a difference for us. The hand of the Father with the word of the Son pushes aside the prosecutor. All the trouble we face may still be there, but we're safe in the Father's hand.

There is a contentment that comes in the middle of trouble. Paul speaks of this when he says, "But we have this treasure in jars of clay, to show that the surpassing power belongs to God and not to us. We are afflicted in every way, but not crushed; perplexed, but not driven to despair; persecuted, but not forsaken; struck down, but not destroyed" (2 Corinthians 4:7–9). In praying "deliver us from evil," we're not asking that all evil would be taken away, for then there would be no cross. It is not a petition of complaint, asking, "Why is this happening to me?" It is finding the Father's hand in the dark and believing that it will be all right.

On my ninth birthday, August 3, 1965, my dad was putting up hay in the barn. Back then, we still put up hay with a sling using long ropes that lifted several bales at once from a wagon. This particular day, when my father pulled on the trip rope to release the load inside the barn, the rope broke. He fell off the hay load and landed on the back of his neck. He got up and walked slowly around, fending off the idea of calling an ambulance. Mom finally persuaded Dad to go to the hospital where they found that he had broken two of the vertebrae in his neck. He was put in traction and ordered to remain in the hospital for at least two weeks. He wouldn't be able to fully work again until the next spring. That night, we could hardly imagine getting through tomorrow's work. Making it to spring seemed impossible.

When my mother came home at 10:30 that night, I was still up, worrying. We had no health insurance, the oats in the fields were ready for harvest in the next two weeks, and after that the corn. We had thirty-five cows to milk every morning and evening, and there was only my mother, my twelve-year-old sister, and my nine-year-old self to do the fieldwork and the milking for the next six months at least. We couldn't do all that. I remember Mom and I talked and cried, and then Mom prayed that somehow help would come. I don't remember now the words she said, but I do remember the feeling that came over me as we ended our prayers. It would be all right.

And it was all right. Two days later, a young man carrying a suitcase walked up our driveway and said, "I heard you need some help." My parents hired Greg, an eighteen-year-old who needed a new home for a year as much as our family needed his help. At harvest time, our neighbors came to harvest the oats for us. Two weeks after the accident, Dad came home to a hospital bed in the living room where he would recover for several more weeks. But by spring, he was back to milking and working in the fields. The answers came one after another after that prayer the first night. Much of my enduring interest in prayer comes from that night's prayer.

Today when we pray, "Deliver us from evil," we might not find ourselves in as dark a spot as my family was that night in 1965—or maybe you feel like the darkness surrounding you is just as bad or worse. Regardless of the darkness we feel around us, our prayer is the same: "Lord, keep us safe in this home until we come to Yours. Make me know Your hand is here." We pray that when answers can't yet be seen, our Father's hand will always be known. Push aside the trouble, fears, and pain so that, even if they are still there, what we know and trust is God's hand. That will make all the difference.

A Hand of Adventure

The Father's hand calms, but it also excites. It preserves our homes even as it leads us to our new one. Think of the excitement of travel, especially when you're not in charge of the itinerary or navigation. Remember the joy of riding in the backseat as you reach your destination and you are responsible for nothing more than folding the map. You simply gaze outside the car's windows in awe of the new landscape you've just entered.

When we pray the Seventh Petition, we're not only content in our Father's hand here; we're also looking for the end of the trip. We want to put this security of the Father into action. We have a journey to complete, from earth to heaven. With every prayer, we're asking the Father to drive us one more mile home. It's like those children camping in the tent of which we spoke earlier. While they can stand another day or two, soon they're going to cry, "Let's go home!" That's the relief and adventure of our prayer.

On one hand, "deliver us from evil" calls for the end of Satan in a flourish of God's power. We're looking for a triumphant crushing of the serpent's head. We've held our breath for this moment ever since Christ rose from the dead. The worst the serpent can do has already been done. Now the Lord's heel is poised over the serpent. The whole Church cries out, "Crush him! Deliver us once and for all." This is the relief that is coming.

On the other hand, there is the ultimate adventure ahead of us. When we're delivered, what joys will come? We can hardly imagine what glory is coming, what freedom from sorrow, and what excitement that only He can bring. This is the unknown trip that we as children can barely see yet eagerly anticipate. Paul can only say that the wonders waiting for us are beyond our experience here: "No eye has seen, nor ear heard, nor the heart of man imagined, what God has prepared for those who love Him" (1 Corinthians 2:9).

Imagine the sights that are waiting for us when we are fully delivered. Before us lies a spent, tired world, but we're about to be taken to another, entirely new world. We can hardly imagine how beautiful it will be. Revelation speaks of what won't be—tears, mourning, death, and any such thing: "They shall hunger no more, neither thirst anymore; the sun shall not strike them, nor any scorching heat. For the Lamb in the midst of the throne will be their shepherd, and He will guide them to springs of living water, and God will wipe away every tear from their eyes" (7:16–17). In that vacuum, we can only imagine what will replace tears and funerals. That is the wonder of our Father's hand taking us upward, saying, "It's time to go home now, to a home you can barely imagine." Soon our time of waiting will be over. Now we snap back and forth the doorknob of heaven, waiting for our Father to take us up. Praying the Lord's Prayer is our eager tug on the Father's sleeve. Our joy is that the Father is just as eager to take us. We know His hand is ready to sweep us home.

CHAPTER EIGHT

{ The Songs We Sing As We Ascend }

NOW THE FATHER HAS US FIRMLY BY THE HAND, AND WE'RE ON OUR WAY HOME. But what shall we talk about when we arrive? Many home-comings have this awkward time right after the expected comments: "How are you?" "How was your trip?" "You sure look good." You're carrying in the bags as you walk up the driveway together. What do you say then? You haven't been home as much as you should. Work has kept you busy and you've been away for quite a while. You don't know the little details of Dad's life that make conversation easy, the questions about whether there's any chicken left over from last night or whether the neighbor's dog has stopped jumping into his yard. So you're left walking up the driveway in this awkward silence, searching for some-thing to say.

If that's how coming home can be for adult children here on earth, what could we possibly say to our heavenly Father as we walk up to Him? We come to our Father's heavenly dwelling, which we've only known through pictures drawn by the Scriptures and by our imag-ination. What do we know of life there? What can we say of our lives that would be of any interest to the God of the universe? His home is a glorious mystery while ours is a boring box. As we come to our Father's home, we're glad for the journey, but we are probably standing before Him awestruck and silent.

The psalmists give us an example of what we can say when we come home to the Father. Psalms 120–134 are each titled "A Song of Ascents." It's likely that these psalms were collected after the Babylo-nian exile to be sung by pilgrims coming to Jerusalem for one of the annual festivals. Many of the songs focus on the joys waiting for them when they reach the court of God. This city, which they perhaps have never seen, has drawn them. "I was glad when they said to me, 'Let us go to the house of the LORD!'" (Psalm 122:1). "Those who trust in the LORD are like Mount Zion, which cannot be moved, but abides forever. As the mountains surround Jerusalem, so the LORD surrounds His people, from this time forth and forevermore" (Psalm 125:1–2). "The LORD bless you from Zion! May you see the prosperity of Jerusalem all the days of your life!" (Psalm 128:5). These psalms stress that Jerusalem is God's appointed place to demonstrate His power and grace. "For the LORD has chosen Zion; He has desired it for His dwelling place: 'This is My resting place forever; here I will dwell, for I have desired it'" (Psalm 132:13–14).

These are the songs of homecoming for the pilgrims to Zion. God reigns on high, His city is in sight, His enemies are crushed, and His mercy brings His own people to His home. These same ideas are a fitting model for our conclusion to the Lord's Prayer. We sing of the kingdom, power, and glory of the Father. His kingdom is before us, and we're being drawn to it by His grace. His power has assured us that we will be delivered from evil. We can hear again the chorus of saints and angels in glory, and just as in the First Petition, we're amazed that our tiny voice is brought into their song as we pray, "For Thine is the kingdom and the power and the glory forever and ever. Amen." These words of kingdom, power, and glory are the songs we sing as we ascend. We can feel them as the three steps upon which our Father is leading us.

His home is a glorious mystery while ours is a boring box.

This conclusion of the Lord's Prayer is also like the Psalms in that it stresses the whole company of believers and travelers singing together. In this conclusion, we are especially conscious of our fellow travelers. It seems inevitable that we focus on our own forgiveness and deliverance from evil during the prayer. It's hard for me to center my request for others' needs when my own are so great. Though we pray that others be delivered from evil, our own dangers demand center stage. But in the Conclusion, we're taken from ourselves and are cast again as pilgrims freed from the day-to-day cares. We're people on a vacation, taken up with a different life. This Conclusion is the briefest of spiritual retreats, bringing us to the foothills of Zion and inviting us to climb to His temple. What is important is the Father, His kingdom, power, and glory, and the sudden realization that we are traveling with so many others far from our ordinary home.

Our other focus is on the Father, His uplifting hand that leads us, and the home to which we're going. Remember, we've just escaped the grasp of the evil one. Feel that involuntary shudder that goes through your shoulders when danger has just passed. Then feel the strength of the Father's hand as He takes you up step-by-step. Perhaps each of the three words (*kingdom*, *power*, and *glory*) might have for you the sensation of being lifted up one more step, as though you are a toddler being lifted by the hand up the stairs—your loving parent holding on tight so you don't fall. So these words remind us that we're on our way upward, toward our new home.

A Song for All of Us to Sing

The Conclusion of the Lord's Prayer is an interesting contrast in that, unlike the previous four petitions, it doesn't refer to us specifically, yet it is a unifying song. The center of attention, which unites all who pray the prayer, is the kingdom, power, and glory of the Father. This becomes a song of victory that brings a celebration among strangers. It's like the buzz that fills the stands those moments when your team wins, fans showing more energy and joy than you've seen in months. It's the spontaneous shout in a stadium when the organ plays those six notes and the fans cry out, "Charge!"

Here in the closing of the prayer, we have the uniting words that draw us from our individual dangers into the victory of the Father. Imagine the scene of the pilgrims returning to Jerusalem and singing the Psalms. They were likely joined by the others on the road. They had never heard the voices of these strangers before. But it didn't matter; the words were universal. When we say the Conclusion of the prayer, notice how the crowd we're with suddenly grows. The words focus on our Father but our peripheral vision scans a stunning sweep of diversity speaking these words. Here an image from Revelation 7:9–10 helps us as John describes the saints in heaven:

> After this I looked, and behold, a great multitude that no one could number, from every nation, from all tribes and peoples and languages, standing before the throne and before the Lamb, clothed in white robes, with palm branches in their hands, and crying out with a loud voice, "Salvation belongs to our God who sits on the throne, and to the Lamb!"

It's easy to imagine this heavenly choir includes in their song the prayer's Conclusion: "For Thine is the kingdom and the power and the glory for ever and ever. Amen." When we began with "Our Father," we saw that the work of Babel was overturned. Though we have thousands of languages today and we can only imagine how we will speak in heaven, at this moment of praying the Lord's Prayer, our English words make perfect sense and blend beautifully with every language from every pocket of earth and heaven. Our Father hears each of us equally and perfectly. Our united sounds are still a symphony with many instruments, but we harmonize beautifully with one another in the Lord's Prayer.

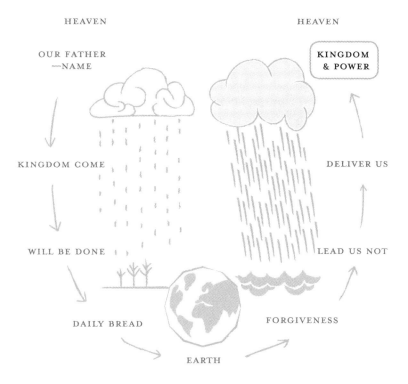

HEAVEN   HEAVEN

OUR FATHER   KINGDOM
—NAME   & POWER

KINGDOM COME   DELIVER US

WILL BE DONE   LEAD US NOT

DAILY BREAD   FORGIVENESS

EARTH

This view of the saints already in heaven is the balance needed for the prayer at its Conclusion. We have traveled a hard road through dry times waiting for bread, through failed times needing forgiveness, and through dangerous times needing deliverance. The end of the prayer lets the saints declare now what will be fully revealed at the end of time. There is the sense here of the conclusion of the Christ-focused praise of Philippians 2:9–11: "Therefore God has highly exalted Him and bestowed on Him the name that is above every name, so that at the name of Jesus every knee should bow, in heaven and on earth and under the earth, and every tongue confess that Jesus Christ is Lord, to the glory of God the Father." When we pray the prayer's Conclusion, we might well remember that not only the saints but every creature, redeemed and lost, will announce the kingdom, power, and glory *From those whose sins are cleansed, white as snow, and even from those whose hearts have been as hard as stones, everyone will acknowledge that He is the Lord.* of the Father and His Son. Our prayer is the smallest beginning of an enormous chorus that acknowledges that the Father has granted to His Son the kingdom, power, and glory. Imagine this avalanche of praise! From those whose sins are cleansed, white as snow, and even from those whose hearts have been as hard as stones, everyone will acknowledge that He is the Lord. This praise will come even from those who have despised the Lord and His prayer while alive. Of course, for those who are condemned, their acknowledgment will be too late for salvation. It will, however, be the truth that even they will have to acknowledge.

A Song That Lifts Our Eyes Upward, Seeing the City

As we look around at this growing choir, praising the risen Lord, we are also drawn upward to His city, the new Jerusalem. One of the most compelling Songs of Ascent is Psalm 121, which begins, "I lift up my eyes to the hills. From where does my help come? My help comes from the LORD, who made heaven and earth." The psalmist takes our eyes off ourselves and the dusty trail leading us over one last hill. We can imagine that this psalm might have been said as Jerusalem first came into view. For miles, the pilgrims have stubbed their toes and kicked up dust. Their feet hurt and their backs ache. Someone must have asked, over and over, "Are we there yet?"

Then someone sees Jerusalem. Its brilliance is so far off in the distance that some scoffer says it's just a mirage. But it really is the city. Now there's no talk of blistered feet or the wrong turn taken yesterday. Imagine this is the first trip to Jerusalem. Here is the city of which you have heard so much. This is the city in which God has placed His temple and said that He would be found by His people. Here we can worship Him, sacrifice, and be assured of forgiveness. Here is the glorious temple where we come into God's presence as we do nowhere else. I imagine that no one suggested we stop for the night out in the hills. No one said, "Well, we've seen it. We might as well go home now." Of all the miles during this trip, these last ones will be the fastest.

As we say the Conclusion of the Lord's Prayer, the new Jerusalem is coming into view. With each step of recalling our Father's kingdom, power, and glory, we see more clearly the majesty that is coming. We see it breaking through the clouds that have hidden it from us. These are the clouds of tears, death, mourning, crying, and pain. But these all are cleared away like a burned-off mist in the new city. That is the view John gives us in his glimpse of the new heaven in Revelation 21:1–4:

> Then I saw a new heaven and a new earth, for the first
> heaven and the first earth had passed away, and the sea was
> no more. And I saw the holy city, new Jerusalem, coming
> down out of heaven from God, prepared as a bride adorned
> for her husband. And I heard a loud voice from the throne
> saying, "Behold, the dwelling place of God is with man. He
> will dwell with them, and they will be His people, and God
> Himself will be with them as their God. He will wipe away
> every tear from their eyes, and death shall be no more,
> neither shall there be mourning, nor crying, nor pain
> anymore, for the former things have passed away.

As we come to the end of the prayer, we see the new city with this same glimpse. It shines with a light undarkened by shadow. Imagine. It is a city without night, with light on every surface, for its light is God Himself: "And night will be no more. They will need no light of lamp or sun, for the Lord God will be their light, and they will reign forever and ever" (Revelation 22:5). This city's shining brilliance comes from no one place but from everywhere, for God shines with His power. When we speak in the prayer about the glory of God, remember this visual glory that is going to surround us in our heavenly home: "And the city has no need of sun or moon to shine on it, for the glory of God gives it light, and its lamp is the Lamb" (Revelation 21:23).

Pray even when YOU'VE BEEN NIBBLING ON THE OLD APPLE.

Imagine going to a fantastic all-you-can-eat buffet restaurant. But instead of filling your plate, you pull out of your pocket a mealy, bruised apple, partially eaten. You nibble on it and try to ignore the awful taste and texture of a rotten piece of fruit. But then you slip it back into your pocket, intending to nibble on it again tomorrow. Ridiculous! How often our days are spent on the mental menu of the old apple, the past bruises, the pieces missing to life. And so Paul says that we are to think on whatever is true, honorable, just, pure, lovely, commendable, excellent, and praiseworthy (Philippians 4:8). Pray to put the apple of old bruises away and make your mental menu today the buffet of God's truth, honor, purity—all that is lovely and excellent.

Look Who Is Here

We see this light by the distant sight of faith, and that light brings also the sound of heaven's chorus. As we pray these concluding words of the Lord's Prayer, we rejoin the chorus that began our prayer. Just as we started the journey in amazement, hallowing the Father's name with the angels and saints, so we hear them again when His throne comes into view and His glory and power are on full display. John's vision of heaven in Revelation 19:1–2, 4–7 repeats the three themes—kingdom, power, and glory—found in our Conclusion of the Lord's Prayer:

After this I heard what seemed to be the loud voice of a great multitude in heaven, crying out, "Hallelujah!

Salvation and glory and power belong to our God, for His judgments are true and just." . . . And the twenty-four elders and the four living creatures fell down and worshiped God who was seated on the throne, saying, "Amen. Hallelujah!" And from the throne came a voice saying, "Praise our God, all you His servants, you who fear Him, small and great." Then I heard what seemed to be the voice of a great multitude, like the roar of many waters and like the sound of mighty peals of thunder, crying out, "Hallelujah! For the Lord our God the Almighty reigns. Let us rejoice and exult and give Him the glory."

Here is the joyous chorus that renews us just as the beginning of the prayer excites us. We start the prayer with a gracious invitation by which we find our words ascending to heaven and to God's ears. But we're modest in that company of saints, angels, the four living creatures beside the throne, and the Father Himself. Who are we to speak in their midst? It's enough to be even the smallest voice within the choir.

But now we've come to the end of the journey. I believe that the prayer has a crescendo throughout its length. We begin with a quiet child's voice, finding a listening Father. We grow in confidence as we take His hand. He comes with us to wait out our droughts and to overwhelm us with forgiveness. He snatches us up onto the rock while temptation's currents rush all around us. There's nothing meek about our cry for forgiveness. Our shout for help in the swirl of temptation is piercing. Now that He has us safe above the tide, it's time to exult. There is, as John hears it, "the loud voice of a great multitude in heaven, crying out" (Revelation 19:1). Notice that mere volume doesn't describe it well enough for John; he also calls on likenesses to nature (19:6), the crowd's voice "like the roar of many waters and like the sound of mighty peals of thunder." Even creation wishes its voice to be a part of this choir.

Remember back to when you've been surrounded by great congregational singing. It was Christmas and you stood to sing "Joy to the World." It was Easter and the processional hymn was "I Know That My Redeemer Lives." When such a crowd of believers sings, you can sing out with all your might and barely hear yourself. You hit the high notes that you mumble over any other day. Everyone sings—even your uncle who never utters a musical note. You barely pause for air, and the only thing wrong with the songs is that they come to an end. This is the way the closing words of the prayer draw us. When you next pray them in a congregation, hear them as a chorus sung with the bass notes of the rushing waters of heaven. Perhaps even see the rushing water as the backdrop for these final notes. We're climbing up beside a waterfall on rocky steps cut into the hillside. As we climb, there is a note and a word for each stone until you reach the three large stones: kingdom, power, and glory. In the background of our song, there is the sound of the waterfall, the rushing water, and the water itself cooling us as we leave the desert. Water has followed us throughout our vision of the prayer, from showers finally coming after droughts to floods of forgiveness and undercurrents of temptation. Here is a benevolent water that cascades down as we go up and laughs with us as we sing of kingdom, power, and glory.

A Bridal Song

This climb beside the waterfall is a vigorous end for our prayer. When we first joined the choir to sing, "Hallowed be Thy name," we wanted to stretch out that moment for its quiet wonder, to drink in the choir and the perfection of being in this holy place—the starting place of the Lord's Prayer: in heaven. Now, in the Conclusion of our prayer, we also want to draw out this moment but for more active reasons. We've seen the handiwork of God, and He has delivered us perfectly into His midst. Revelation 19:7–8 shows us as perfect in His sight: "For the marriage of the Lamb has come, and His bride has made herself ready; it was granted her to clothe herself with fine linen, bright and pure."

Even though our journey in the prayer has been difficult and has gone through the lowest places in our lives, complete with failure and persistent temptation, remember how He sees you as you sing the final words of your prayer. The saints before Him, both here on earth and in heaven, are His Bride. Paul well describes the Bride in Ephesians 5:25–27: "Christ loved the church and gave Himself up for her, that He might sanctify her, having cleansed her by the washing of water with the word, so that He might present the church to Himself in splendor, without spot or wrinkle or any such thing, that she might be holy and without blemish." We finish the prayer as the freshly washed Church.

169

The sins we just spoke of are as impossible to find as the water molecules that splashed over the waterfall five minutes ago. The rushing water beside us in these final words reminds us of the constant cleansing that washes us as we approach His Kingdom. His power is the resurrection of His Son who welcomes us into His glory as His own Bride.

Kingdom, power, and glory are witnesses to the character of the groom. They reassure the Bride of His care and the life that is coming. It is like the transformation of Elizabeth's affections in Jane Austen's *Pride and Prejudice*, a book most of us probably read in one English class or another. Perhaps you remember the story—Elizabeth meets Mr. Darcy, a rich but seemingly proud man, who says he loves her and wishes to marry her despite her dislike of him. She refuses him but then is drawn by curiosity to visit his estate when she believes him to be absent. There she is moved by the beauty of the house, the love of the housekeeper for Mr. Darcy's kindness, and upon his unexpected arrival, Mr. Darcy's own gracious manner toward her. When she sees the splendor of the house and its magnificent grounds, Elizabeth remembers her rejection of Mr. Darcy and reflects, "'And of this place,' thought she, 'I might have been mistress! With these rooms I might now have been familiarly acquainted! Instead of viewing them as a stranger, I might have rejoiced in them as my own, and welcomed to them as visitors my uncle and aunt.'"[23] When she reflects on Darcy's kindness to herself and her aunt and uncle, she is astonished. She has rejected him and now is found trespassing on his property. Yet, he is kind, and she can think of only one reason: he still loves her. For that, she felt gratitude,

Water has followed us throughout our vision of the prayer, from showers finally coming after droughts, floods of forgiveness, and undercurrents of temptation. Here is a benevolent water that cascades down as we go up and laughs with us as we sing of kingdom, power, and glory.

23 Jane Austen, *Pride and Prejudice* (New York: The Century Company, 1903), 205–6.

gratitude, not merely for [him] having once loved her, but for loving her still well enough to forgive all the petulance and acrimony of her manner in rejecting him, and all the unjust accusation accompanying her rejection. He who, she had been persuaded, would avoid her as his greatest enemy, seemed, on this accidental meeting, most eager to preserve the acquaintance. . . . Such a change in a man of so much pride excited not only astonishment but gratitude—for to love, ardent love, it must be attributed.[24]

Isn't our approach to the majestic home of the Father much the same? We come to the Father whom we have rejected and toward whom we have behaved with ingratitude and selfishness. We have seen just a glimpse of His kingdom, power, and glory; we've overheard the praise gladly given Him by His servants, the angels and saints. We would, like Elizabeth, love to be in this house of His, but the thought of being His bride goes beyond our dreams. Who are we that He would think kindly of us? Isn't our envy of His servants proof of our selfishness again? Shouldn't He, as Mr. Darcy might have done, avoid us as His greatest enemy?

But He receives us with astonishing grace. When we suddenly come to His doorstep in the Lord's Prayer, He throws open the door. He welcomes us in, seats us with His own, and then gives us the tour of His kingdom. We can only stumble out a few words about the glory and power we see, but all the while we must wonder how He can be so gracious to us. Then He washes us, clothes us in beautiful white garments, and sets us before the host in His home as His own Bride. This is the amazing welcome we have throughout the entire prayer. Now at the Conclusion, we recite for ourselves and our brothers and sisters the wonders of His kingdom, His power, and His glory.

This joy is immediate. Our Father has a kingdom, power, and glory that already shine. We see it in a distance, but it is a fixed kingdom. The pilgrims knew Jerusalem waited before them. So our Father's kingdom already stands before us. His glory and His power radiate from it. In a prayer filled with imperatives, asking that God would act and in which we must often make our petition and wait, the Conclusion of the prayer is a welcome indicative statement—there is no

24 Austen, *Pride and Prejudice*, 222–23.

unfulfilled wish about the kingdom; our asking about the kingdom has been covered already in the Second Petition. Here there is only declaration. Our Father's kingdom and power and glory are already His, and He has extended them to us, His Bride.

GROW THE RICHES YOU DO HAVE

"One pretends to be rich, yet has nothing; another pretends to be poor, yet has great wealth" (Proverbs 13:7). Not every garden is in the front yard or in a raised bed. Some people hide their gardens in their backyards, say little about them, and yet eat well all summer. As we close the Lord's Prayer, we have found the garden of the very words of prayer, known to some and hidden from others. Our own words, said with vanity only, would be an empty plot. But the words of the Lord's Prayer, hidden in the quiet moments of our lives, bring actual riches. Lord, let me be authentically rich in repeating Your words today.

A Marching Song

One of the most remarkable men I have ever met could sing while he ran. He was the drill instructor for our army training company in Fort Monmouth, New Jersey. This person was the healthiest, most energetic man I've ever known. He conducted physical training sessions all day—in the steaming heat of a New Jersey summer no less. Our company trained with him in the late afternoon when the PT grounds were a shadeless sauna. After a half hour of push-ups and sit-ups, done in more variations than I had ever dreamed possible, we ran. The run would last for half an hour or so, and when we ran as a unit, he ran beside us, setting the pace. What was remarkable was his tireless singing, one army marching song after the next. He sang each line first and we all sang it back. This man was in his midthirties, older than most of us, and he had been working and running all day prior to our training session. Yet, he could run and sing out in a voice that carried over forty or more men, while we, on the other hand, could only mumble, pant, or say nothing at all. He continued to sing out every line, so loud that forty huffing men could hear it. And he did it. Day after day, he never stopped. He never said, "I'm too hot, too tired, and you people are too slow. The army's not worth this." He ran and he sang. And when we listened to him and watched the way he ran, we were encouraged to do the same. We ran because this man's energy lifted an entire company of tired men who thought they were completely spent.

This is just one example of what can happen when we're ready to give up. But the right words become infectious and give more power than they take. "Thine is the kingdom and the power and the glory forever and ever." These words, like an ancient march, tie us with people who have gone long before us. Hundreds of thousands of men and women have sung the army's songs; millions and millions have learned our Father's song. The army's songs took us back to the barracks. The Lord's Prayer takes us home where our family is gathered. The words of the Lord's Prayer promise that there is a place in His kingdom for us, and there are treasures that wait for our taking when we come. His kingdom, power, and glory have not been picked over or trampled by the careless. Our journey is not worthless. His kingdom, power, and glory are a fixed mark that no one can remove. These words come from the tireless pioneer of our faith, who has gone before us and calls them out for our repeating. When we conclude our prayer this way, we're an echo of the race He has already run.

I hope that these images enliven the Conclusion of the Lord's Prayer for you. The Conclusion is the call to follow upward to the home and the glory that He has prepared for us. There is no exhaustion to these words, only the renewing that they bring. His kingdom, power, and glory draw us up.

One Final Note

I'm not a big fan of songs that simply fade away after the fourth repetition of the chorus. It seems like someone in the sound booth said, after hearing three choruses, "Well, that's about enough," and slowly turned down the sound. I imagine the singers going on for another minute or two while the technicians turn out the lights and head out for lunch. I prefer a song that ends, and everyone knows it. Raise the volume, hit the high note, crash the symbol, call it done. When you finish, don't leave us guessing.

The Lord's Prayer comes to a cymbal-crashing end with "Amen." Here are confidence and certainty. Luther said of "Amen" at the end of the prayer: "This is nothing else than the word of undoubting faith, which does not pray on a dare but knows that God does not lie to him [Titus 1:2]. For He has promised to grant it" (Large Catechism, Part III, paragraph 120). Here is certainty. We have come to our Father's home and have heard His promise that we should pray these words. If we were to pray only our words, perhaps we would be like singers who never know when to end. When have we said enough? How many endless choruses should we repeat to get His attention? How loud should we be to reach Him? But here we have His own words and the final one says we have done nothing but follow His command. We have said His words, and He promises He will do His work.

"Amen" is saying "I'm home!"

When we come to the end of the Lord's Prayer, remember how we began. We spoke in the chapter on the Introduction of the prayer about coming home to our Father's house where the lights are always on. When I came home at night to the farm, the lights were on because Mom and Dad were home. I never had to timidly open the door, like some intruding guest, and ask, "Is anyone home?" as though I needed permission to go further. No, I just came in, and after the screen door slapped shut, I'd yell, "I'm home!"

"Amen" is saying "I'm home!" "Amen" knows the Father is home. "Amen" knows that He's heard everything we've said in the prayer while we were still coming up the driveway and the front walk. "Amen" is not "good-bye." When we've completed the prayer, we've just arrived at home again with the Father. The words may end, but who's going to end their visit after just seventy words? We just got here. Now is the time to reflect on the Father's words. Repeat the petitions and bask in the company of saints and angels. See how every petition is seconded by the Son to the Father and how warmly He says your name. Our Father has drawn us in by His light. "Amen" says "We're home."

CHAPTER NINE

{ Looking Back over the Journey }

THINK BACK ON A TRIP YOU RECENTLY TOOK. It could be one that lasted a few hours or a day, a week or most of a month. What do you remember? Most of the details have probably faded away, but you probably remember certain scenes, words, and feelings. Perhaps you remember that view from the mountain one morning as the fog lifted or that time you suddenly saw a bald eagle. While many of us take long videos of our trips, I suspect that few of those videos ever get replayed, at least in their entirety. We remember trips moment by moment, flipping pictures before our eyes.

We've been on a long trip through the Lord's Prayer. This book is like a video of the journey through the prayer, and I suspect that no one will replay every scene that we've recorded in their entirety. But I hope that some moments do stand out for you. I especially hope that the overall idea of a journey illustrates your praying of the Lord's Prayer. This journey makes the prayer a connected whole, and the images connect it to your own experiences. The prayer is more than a separate part of our lives, a closet we enter at the end of the day. It can be in the center of our experiences and feelings. Day after day we'll recognize the prayer when we see a house with its front-porch light beaming brightly, when we hear of parents waiting up for their teenager to return home, when we see a drought-withered cornfield or a child floating on her pink raft, or when we notice a father catching his daughter by the hand just before she falls on the ice. We see and live the Lord's Prayer as much as we say it.

This closing chapter will lay out the most significant pictures of our journey through the prayer. Yes, they will be some of the same pictures we've already seen, but overall this chapter ties together the journey with new images. I hope this brings together the whole trip in a unified way. Second, I suggest ways in which you might make this journey more personal for you by changing some of these images to fit your own experiences. Finally, I offer ways in which you can pray more often with the Lord's Prayer as your foundation and guide. While there's no right or wrong way to pray the Lord's Prayer, these ideas might help you to pray more often and with clearer ties to your life and the world around you.

The Photo Album—From Home and Back Again

We began with an image of home with the lights on. When we pray the Lord's Prayer, we should start at our Father's home. The image that draws us in is our Father's home and the warmth and light that pour from Him. The Father's gracious invitation to address Him as "Father" and to find Him at home is what draws us to pray. It's true that we have His command to pray and for that reason alone we should say the words of the Lord's Prayer each day. But I'm afraid that we might make praying the prayer a spiritual exercise only, no more exciting or inviting than brushing our teeth because we eventually have to face the dentist. But the Lord's Prayer calls us to itself because it brings us home. It gives us a welcome we don't deserve but can't refuse. In its very first words, "Our Father who art in heaven," the prayer shows our Father standing at the door looking for us. Behind Him, His light and warmth invite us in. The prayer begins with the honor of being His children and of calling Him Father. This in itself is so rich a gift that it both overwhelms whatever else we might ask and assures us that we will receive what we ask.

The centerpiece of the prayer is approaching our Father's home and being drawn to Him. In our coming to the Father and His home in the very opening of the prayer, it seems that we've ended the journey in the first mile. We've already arrived where we want to be. The First Petition has an element of a homecoming celebration when we pray, "Hallowed be Thy name." We've come into the choir room of the Father and are given a part to sing. No petition of the prayer has such a degree of wonder as this. As sinful creatures, we might almost expect to call out to Him, to pray for forgiveness, and to ask for food and protection. We, of course, would want His kingdom and will to be done, but right at the beginning of the prayer, we're reminded that our words are actually heard and that they have a part in hallowing and praising His perfect name. We might imagine that we would be allowed to listen to the angels and saints as they sing. We might dream that a bit of quiet humming along would be all right, as long as no one else can hear us. This is the most that we might expect.

But when we pray to our Father in heaven, we're immediately ushered into His hearing so that as He hears the perfect choir of heaven, He hears us. He blends our song about His perfect name with the angels and saints in heaven, who are already praising Him. He ushers us into their ranks, hands us the music, and says, "Sing!" Here is the amazing result: we somehow harmonize with the praise that already surrounds Him. Our words are perfectly acceptable to Him because He hears each of us as though He were listening to His own Son. The Son who

> *But the Lord's Prayer calls us to itself because it brings us home. It gives us a welcome we don't deserve but can't refuse.*

intercedes for us also gives us His own voice. He speaks for us, and when we speak, we sound like Him to the Father. What parent, listening to the choir performance of his or her child, doesn't say, "That was wonderful!"? So we come to our Father, sounding like His children. If ever there was a petition to savor, to repeat for the joy of its own melody, it's the first. This beginning reminds us that prayer is not our own daring work, for in prayer, we join in the chorus that has been going on forever.

No Stopping—Keep Moving

In every journey, there are places where you wish you could just stop. It's that town where every house is charming and picturesque, the weather is perfect, and your quaint hotel is situated on a beautiful street. You imagine saying something like, "Why don't we stop living out of a suitcase? Who wants to climb into the van anymore? Let's settle down here." But you never actually do it. You don't go to the real estate agent or start inquiring about a new mortgage. You've got to go back. Work's waiting. Your neighbors are only going to care for your beagle two more days. The kids have school starting next week. Stop dreaming and start driving.

In the Lord's Prayer, we come to the same point between the First and Second Petitions. We would love to go no farther than our Father's home. Why not simply stay put and sing with the choir and praise His name? Given the First Petition, we might expect that our next petition would be the final prayer of the Bible: "Amen. Come, Lord Jesus!" (Revelation 22:20). All we want is the end of this age and our permanent rest with the saints. We want heaven's song to go on with us in the center of the choir. But the prayer goes back to work and takes us with it. The prayer wakes us up to the world that's waiting.

"Thy kingdom come, Thy will be done on earth as it is in heaven" are the words of a little girl taking her father's hand. She leads him to where her work is waiting. She can't do it alone, and she doesn't want to do it alone. So she takes his hand and says, "You come too." Here is the warmth of the Father's first greeting at the doorway of heaven, but now this warmth comes with us. And even better than sending just the warmth, He brings Himself.

On every family trip, my wife and I like to buy or find a souvenir. It's the seashell from New Jersey, that odd red rock from the Badlands, and the plastic dolphin from the Marineland show that cause us to relive wonderful memories. I understand souvenirs and have lots of them, but there's something sad about them. They try to capture a trip and hold it one place. But trips are winds; they blow over the land and are gone. You can't hold the wind and still have it move you.

He is the God of the fertile garden. But He comes to claim even the parched earth as His.

That's why, in the journey of the Lord's Prayer, we ask the Father to come with us. We've come to Him in heaven. We've sung His praise, yet now we have to go back. But we want the Father to go back with us. It won't do simply to have a gift, some heavenly souvenir, even if it's bread or forgiveness. We want to bring with us the heart of our trip, which is the Father Himself. We ask for His kingdom and His will to be done so that He will bring these to us Himself.

It is the dream of almost everyone to visit a beloved grandparent. Imagine when you were young saying to your grandfather, "Why don't you come home with us?" What if he said, "Glad to!" He packs in ten minutes and climbs in the car. You would be absolutely astonished. He's coming with us! "Of course," he says. "You asked. And I was planning to come anyway. I was just waiting for you to ask." So our Father comes with us to deliver His kingdom and His will. But better than sending these alone, He brings Himself too. He always intends to come but He waits for us to ask so that we'll know when He's coming. The key in the Second and Third Petitions is our taking of the Father's hand and saying, "You come too."

Now We're at This Home Again

When we come to the Fourth Petition, our Father has come home with us. But our house needs work, and we might be inclined to start by explaining why it's the way it is. Oh, the excuses we would have! But our Father simply gives us these words to say: "Give us this day our daily bread." He invites us to ask for the gifts He's ready to bestow upon us. Daily bread brings all our needs under one name. But before His gifts come into sight, perhaps all we see is the drought. Our world is dry. Deep, long cracks are the only things growing in our soil. So we're not asking for a whole month's supply of bread, just what can fall to us today. Perhaps we'll still be waiting through today for some of this bread. The drought might linger, but we'll have enough to get through today. Still, as we wait, we know it's all right because our Father has come. We might wonder why He would come where there is a drought. He is the God of the fertile garden. But He comes to claim even the parched earth as His. While we wait for the full rain to fall, He tells us of the droughts He's known before this. Our drought and need are nothing new to Him; He has always brought daily bread to His people.

Then, just as we are waiting for today's shower, the flood comes. Probably the most remembered part of any trip is when the car was almost hit, when the storm flattened the tent, or when you thought you lost your child in the theme park. It's that moment when you're about to be swept away. That moment when getting to the front of the McDonald's line or finding a motel with a pool doesn't matter. The trip is a success if you just survive the moment.

In the same way, the peak of the journey through the Lord's Prayer is the flood of forgiveness that overwhelms us. When we pray for forgiveness, it comes with a torrent that pushes aside our other worries. Our need for forgiveness is the crisis that strangely waits until now—the middle of our journey—to strike. We might have thought it would come in the first mile with our Father. But it comes now, in the middle of the journey. By the middle of the journey, He's found us as we truly are. Our short tempers and our selfish tendencies have burst out like dandelions on a parched lawn. Given a little drought, the grass fades, but the dandelions flourish. Our drought has been long enough that the weeds of bitterness and desperation are everywhere. He can't miss them. Every step with us finds Him standing over another of our trespasses. We can only cry out, "Forgive us."

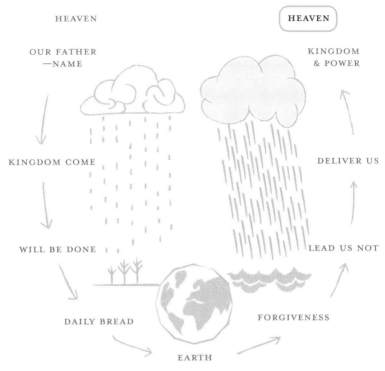

HEAVEN

HEAVEN

OUR FATHER
—NAME

KINGDOM
& POWER

KINGDOM COME

DELIVER US

WILL BE DONE

LEAD US NOT

DAILY BREAD

FORGIVENESS

EARTH

His forgiveness is His overwhelming flood. What a remarkable flood forgiveness is. It buries our sins while it waters the seeds of faith He has planted. It raises up a new life while it drowns an old. There is such an abundance to this forgiving flood while it saturates us. During the drought, our neighbor wonders if we have some water to spare. "Of course," we say, "take all you want. I'll even bring some over. Don't worry, I have way more than I need; and besides, every time I get rid of it more shows up." The crisis passes with a strange peace. The old weeds are buried, and the old footsteps of trespassing are covered over. A green garden is laid down, and our Father is walking through it with us in the cool of the evening.

Time to Turn toward Home

You would think this is the perfect moment in the trip—the time when we head home. The Father is with us and has covered our sins. We've gotten His gifts, and they've covered us completely. But like most perfect moments, they last only an instant. While we can ask, "Why should this ever change?" it already has started to change. The Garden of Eden came with perfection and yet was surprisingly the scene for temptation. And so the washing of forgiveness leads us to call for protection from temptation. Temptation comes in those peaceful moments when we're basking like children on their rafts, floating on the tide. We've missed the undercurrents beneath us and the waves building beyond us. All these threaten to overturn us in a depth we can't handle. What we need is a Father who will bring us to shore before the waves overtake us. We need a Father who will call us in before the lightning strikes. We need a Father who takes us firmly by the hand.

When He takes our hand, He tells us, "It's time to come home." This is the crucial turning point of the trip when we realize that, for all that we've seen and done, it would be best if we went home. Most every trip has to end. The best trips make you glad to leave but even happier to return home again. The Father's outstretched hand, beckoning us, reaching back for us—this is the best invitation to come home with our Father, who's walking ahead of us. He's crushed our old enemy so that nothing can separate us from His love. Remember that though we walk through dangers that try to imprison us, they have no power since we've already heard the verdict of the Judge over us. We are not guilty! Now we can return home.

Perhaps the most satisfying steps in a trip are the last three to the front door. The door swings open and everything is in good order. These last steps come in the Conclusion of the prayer as we see the Father's kingdom, power, and glory. Here are the words that no longer ask for gifts but celebrate that this kingdom, power, and glory are already the Father's. These words take up the melody of the angel choir we heard in the beginning. Once more we've come to the threshold of heaven, and the choir includes our words with theirs. This song comes to a triumphant end with "Amen." There's no doubt and no hesitation in the prayer. We end with the Father opening the door just as we began. The light and warmth that welcomed us in the beginning take us in again.

Your Own Journey

Many of these images of praying the Lord's Prayer are unique to my own experiences, but I hope they've been helpful to you. However, there are likely some that have little connection to you. You can imagine motorcycle racing and droughts on a farm, but you might relate better to sailboats on a calm sea or layoffs in an auto plant. In this section, I'm encouraging you to do just that. Imagine the experiences you have had that animate the petitions of the prayer.

The journey of the prayer in this way is a bit like a group tour. For example, we all get on the same plane, fly to Miami, get on a cruise ship, sail for seven days, and then fly home. We all went on the same trip. But ask us individually how the trip was and our answers will be amazingly different. One of us was sick from the second day on, stayed in the cabin most of the voyage, and was amazed at how good the chicken soup was. Another one of us found love, paid little attention to the food, and can't stop talking about the new budding romance.

What are the images that enliven the prayer as you say it? Of course, they don't make the prayer something other than itself. They are only the natural trappings that come to us when we say, "Our Father." They are your personal experiences with prayer so that when you say, "Amen," you have a past that says, "It will be so."

My first suggestion is that you pray the Lord's Prayer, its entire journey, and think of the parallel experiences you have. I hope that your childhood home was a warm, welcoming place to which you could always return. I hope that you can recall the particular smells and sounds that met you when you came home. Remember the different times you came home, as a child from kindergarten, as a teenager in trouble, as a new couple from your first home, or as a parent bringing the first grandchild home.

When you come to the praises of the heavenly choir in the First Petition, perhaps you are already a talented singer. This idea of singing with the angels is more fulfillment of your dreams than the near nightmare it is for me. But perhaps singing is not a powerful image for you at all. The idea of holiness and our participation with the saints and angels reminds me also of a restoration of perhaps a centuries-old painting. Here is the master's work, carefully attended to by his trained assistants. Suddenly you come, and instead of shouldering you aside, they open their ranks, give you a brush, and tell you to get busy. The work of hallowing the name and work of the Father goes on with the saints and angels, and in our prayer, we join them.

Robert Frost's poem of clearing the spring and fetching the calf may not draw you in as it does me in connection with the Third and Fourth Petitions. You likely haven't run into the two baby birds that met me that one morning. But what images work for you? The theme is "You come too." Perhaps your story is dramatic, such as the time you were in the hospital and your mother literally stayed beside you for days. Or your father was your partner in adventures—mountain climbing or flying—where you were part of an adult world though still very young. Either way, remember these as images that color your saying of the petitions, "Thy kingdom come, Thy will be done on earth as it is in heaven."

After we ask our Father to come with us, we then stand waiting for daily bread. I know not many people grow up on a farm, but you can imagine a drought without living through it. When have you waited desperately for a good that you knew was there, but which simply hadn't yet come? You waited for your child to come home, the doctor to call with the test results, or the mail to include that check you so desperately needed. Here I hope you remember the feeling of trust in tension. Your child, your test, your check were all on their way, but when were they going to arrive? This is the Fourth Petition. Our trust in our Father feels the tension of waiting each evening before the new morning's bread falls.

> *When have you waited desperately for a good that you knew was there, but which simply hadn't yet come?*

The rarity of the farm is perhaps matched by the flood. Not everyone has had the opportunity to watch water make an island of their home. I know also that this matching of forgiveness with a flood might be puzzling since forgiveness is only kindness and a flood is a careless cruelty. But the flood's abundance, the covering of tracks, and the eagerness to share the floodwater with anyone—these aspects give flood imagery meaning for the Lord's Prayer.

You may have your own image in mind when you pray, "Forgive us our trespasses as we forgive those who trespass against us." When has there been a sudden turn in your life, a new relationship, a new job, an adopted child, something that was completely beyond your expectations? You had given up hope for this, perhaps never even dreamed it, and now it has come. This gift turns your world around. You find yourself humming, even though you never hum. A gift of life-changing worth has come, so you want to invite the world to share it with you.

In the closing images of danger and rescue, some scenes should be familiar to most of us. My stories about the men who helped me fix my old Ford cars may bring back similar memories for many of you. But even if your cars have always had fuel injection, air conditioning, and a Bluetooth connection to your smartphone, you know the need for a mentor. You remember the first days of junior high, the frightening first night in a college dorm, or the first day of basic training. Who will befriend you out of all these strangers? Who is genuine, and who is just sizing you up? Remember the relief when it was clear that there was someone who would catch you and whose hand would always be there. Those are the images that enliven your requests, "Lead us not into temptation, but deliver us from evil."

Finally, the journey comes to an end. Let your images of the end have a Jerusalem-like quality. Remember seeing something for the first time, though you had pictured it a thousand times? Perhaps for you, it was the first trip to the Rockies when you had grown up in Iowa. When we say, "Thine is the kingdom and the power and the glory," we're coming to the Father's city with its majesty spilling over us. We're not there yet, but by faith, we can see its peaks.

Then say, "Amen." The song of the journey comes to a triumphant end. Think of your favorite songs, those with definitive endings, whether they're Sousa marches or something more soothing. Think of those songs that trigger your memories of road trips, driving to work, washing dishes, or putting children to sleep. But whatever the song, remember an ending that both completes the song and leaves you wanting to start it all over. To match "Amen," we need an ending that immediately makes you start humming the song over again without thinking, and later has you trying to remember the words to the second verse. "Amen" is our homecoming, as much beginning as ending, the end of our words but not of our Father's. It is the final step of a journey and also the beginning of our visit with the Father.

When thinking of the journey of the prayer, there might be other images that make a particular match for you. One of the most obvious is the smell of fresh bread when speaking the Fourth Petition. Linger over the bread machine in the kitchen, walk to the bakery down the street, stand in front of the deli in the morning, or park in front of the bagel shop. Don't go near the day-old or discounted bread. Don't take out that bagel that has been in your freezer for two weeks and is now a petrified round. You want authentic, no preservatives, fresh today bread. You want bread that's made for today and brings you back tomorrow. That's the point of the Fourth Petition. We pray for the Father's bread that comes only today but which leaves us waiting for tomorrow's bread overnight.

Other images that enliven our prayers might be the situations of movies, television, and books that you encounter. I used *Pride and Prejudice* in chapter 8. Perhaps others have already come to your mind throughout the book. Perhaps it's Mark Twain's *Life on the Mississippi*. As Mark Twain learns to be a riverboat pilot on the Mississippi, he must come to know every bend and crossing in the river by heart. What he must also learn is to trust what he knows despite any evidence or doubt to the contrary. In one famous episode, the pilot who is training him tests him by having false readings called out, suggesting that the boat was about to run aground. Twain panicked, called for the engines to stop, and tried to back up. But the river was deeper than deep at that point and Twain knew it—or should have known it.

"Didn't you *know* there was no bottom in that crossing?"

"Yes, sir, I did."

"Very well, then. You shouldn't have allowed me or anybody else to shake your confidence in that knowledge. Try to remember that."[25]

We are all Twain at times. We know, or we should know, the limitless love and care of God. And yet the troubled, ruffled waters around us whisper that we're in trouble, about to crash. Forgetting what we know and fearing these imagined shallows, how often we throw up the wheel and try to back up. The prayer is our call to the Father that we would not forget the depth of His love and His constant hand on us. "Lord, the water around us is troubled but in the depths is Your constant love."

The depth of our security lies with His Son. He has fallen so we can be lifted up. The Father has allowed the worst to strike Him. A dead tree snagged His very life. There is an awe to our speaking the

25   Mark Twain, *Life on the Mississippi* (New York: P. F. Collier & Son Company, 1917), 117.

line, "Deliver us from evil," when we see the Son falling to His death. Then when we are lifted up, there is the same Son, at the very top, safe, whole, victorious. This is the tension of our prayer, seeing both the falling Savior and the ascended Son.

These are just a few ways in which we can greet the Lord's Prayer every day. It becomes a two-way street: we pray and so think of the experiences and needs that the prayer addresses; we read, watch a movie, or listen to a song and admire the words and characters who recall for us the prayer. Each of our lives is a setting for the gem of the Lord's Prayer. By the particular way in which God has made us, we each hold the same prayer but we turn different facets of it to the light. You give the prayer a distinct turn so that in your life others see more of the Father's holiness, His forgiveness, and His rescue. The prayer is lived as much as it's said.

Living Out the Prayer

The Lord's Prayer can be prayed in ways that reflect the many different situations in which we live. To start, I encourage you to pray the prayer often during the day just as the prayer is written. It might serve as the beginning for your time of prayer. It could be the start of that commute into work when you know that you've got half an hour by yourself to think and pray. The prayer is the beginning for your own prayers that follow. Here we use the "Amen" of the Lord's Prayer as our beginning, our way of saying "I'm home." Then we continue the conversation with our Father.

The prayer is also a wonderful summary of what you've been praying at night before falling asleep or during your commute to work. In that half hour, you've probably been both praying and wandering a bit in your thoughts. Then you see the exit coming that means you have only two minutes left until you arrive at your destination. Say the Lord's Prayer as a way to focus your previous thoughts. Even if the last twenty-five minutes have been a jumble of pious thoughts and grocery lists, here are seventy true words that are the definition of prayer.

Additionally, I think that the Lord's Prayer can also stand to be expanded and shortened. It is good to begin with the Lord's Prayer when we pray, but to do so slowly, letting each petition lead us on its own tangents. Dwell on the Father, His heavenly home, and His name. Then come back to His kingdom and will after listening to the angels sing for a time. Take the time you need to confess and recount your trespasses and pour the flood of forgiveness over your neighbor. Linger over each of the final steps that take us to "Amen."

This extended praying allows for the sort of images that have made up much of this book. It's the time for the recalling of Bible passages and accounts that apply to the prayer. The beauty of the prayer as a journey is that each side trip doesn't end the overall journey. We're recalled to the central task by the next petition. We know that the end of the prayer is a welcome into our Father's home. Our own wanderings, our recalled trespasses, our fears over today's drought of bread or the fierceness of our enemies are all matched by the certainty of our rescue from evil into our Father's kingdom, glory, and power.

"Amen" is our homecoming, as much beginning as ending, the end of our words but not of our Father's.

This long praying of the prayer has a companion in short prayers, which use one or two petitions of the prayer. I often find that a word from someone, a particular scene in a television show, a headline in the paper makes me think of one of the petitions of the Lord's Prayer. It seems perfectly right to use that petition by itself at that time without saying the entire prayer. The whole prayer is assumed when we simply pray "Hallowed be thy name" after we've sung a hymn such as "Praise to the Lord, the Almighty." When you open the mail and more bills than checks have come again, "give us this day our daily bread" is certainly a fitting thought. Can you really ask to be forgiven when you did "it" again? Your promises to change had barely stopped echoing in heaven before they were broken again. "Forgive us our trespasses" is the only hope we have. With the Lord's Prayer, we have more than our own words or presumptions. The Lord's Prayer is His command to pray and His promise to answer. Here are words that are given to every sinner who hopes to pray. These words are the foundation for all that you're about to say, and they are enough when they're all you say. Pray, then, for deliverance from temptation and evil and say "Amen." In these ways, the prayer meets us in a dozen moments every day.

Words to Take Us Home

This journey through the Lord's Prayer has been a long trip. I hope it has done the two things a good trip should do. First, it should give you moments to remember and relive through its pictures and words. Second, it should give you the incentive to travel again. A good trip is never done. It's traveled again with every memory, recalling the shrimp you ate at that restaurant overlooking the water, the thunderstorm in New Jersey, and the sunset that last evening of your beach vacation. A good trip is never done because it's the reason we travel again. It reincarnates itself in our next trip and is so lively that even if that second trip is a disaster, there'll be another after that.

> *Even if the last twenty-five minutes have been a jumble of pious thoughts and grocery lists, here are seventy true words that are the definition of prayer.*

I hope that you've found this to be a good trip. Perhaps you have seven or eight snapshots in mind that capture the journey we've taken. You can see the Father's bright home, the angels moving aside to take you into the choir, the child taking her Father's hand, the rain clouds moving in from the west, the floodwater washing everything away, our Father catching us up before the wave swamps our raft, and our Father saying, "It's time to come home." Perhaps the images I've mentioned have already made new ones for you. "Come home." That's a trip waiting to be taken. I suspect that this journey will continue to change throughout our lives. We move, our family dynamics change, our work comes and goes, friends and family members pass away. These are the new trips that the prayer is going to take with us. We are never done with this journey.

God bless your travel through the Lord's Prayer. May it be a lifetime of asking with the disciples, "Teach us to pray," and hearing Jesus say these familiar words, "When you pray, say . . ." (Luke 11:1–2). When we say the words of the Lord's Prayer, we're still asking Him to teach us how to pray. May these words be a well-worn path for you. May they take you to sights and sounds you've never seen or heard before. Finally, may they take you and all the saints on earth to your Father's home.